SEDUCING THE DEMON

ALSO BY ERICA JONG

POETRY

Fruits & Vegetables

Half-Lives

Loveroot

At the Edge of the Body

Ordinary Miracles

Becoming Light

FICTION

Fear of Flying

How to Save Your Own Life

*Fanny: Being the True History of the Adventures
of Fanny Hackabout-Jones*

Megan's Book of Divorce; Megan's Two Houses

Parachutes & Kisses

Serenissima: A Novel of Venice
(republished as *Shylock's Daughter*)

Any Woman's Blues

Inventing Memory

Sappho's Leap

NONFICTION

Witches

The Devil at Large: Erica Jong on Henry Miller

Fear of Fifty

What Do Women Want?

SEDUCING THE DEMON

Writing for My Life ERICA JONG

JEREMY P. TARCHER/PENGUIN   *a member of Penguin Group (USA) Inc.*   NEW YORK

JEREMY P. TARCHER/PENGUIN
Published by the Penguin Group
Penguin Group (USA) Inc., 375 Hudson Street, New York, New York 10014, USA •
Penguin Group (Canada), 90 Eglinton Avenue East, Suite 700, Toronto, Ontario
M4P 2Y3, Canada (a division of Pearson Penguin Canada Inc.) • Penguin Books
Ltd, 80 Strand, London WC2R 0RL, England • Penguin Ireland, 25 St Stephen's
Green, Dublin 2, Ireland (a division of Penguin Books Ltd) • Penguin Group
(Australia), 250 Camberwell Road, Camberwell, Victoria 3124, Australia
(a division of Pearson Australia Group Pty Ltd) • Penguin Books India Pvt Ltd,
11 Community Centre, Panchsheel Park, New Delhi–110 017, India • Penguin
Group (NZ), Cnr Airborne and Rosedale Roads, Albany, Auckland 1310, New
Zealand (a division of Pearson New Zealand Ltd) • Penguin Books (South Africa)
(Pty) Ltd, 24 Sturdee Avenue, Rosebank, Johannesburg 2196, South Africa

Penguin Books Ltd, Registered Offices:
80 Strand, London WC2R 0RL, England

Most Tarcher/Penguin books are available at special quantity discounts for bulk pur-
chase for sales promotions, premiums, fund-raising, and educational needs. Special
books or book excerpts also can be created to fit specific needs. For details, write Penguin Group (USA) Inc. Special Markets, 375 Hudson Street, New York, NY 10014.

Library of Congress Cataloging-in-Publication Data
Jong, Erica.
Seducing the demon : writing for my life / by Erica Jong.
p.   cm.
ISBN 1-58542-444-7
1. Jong, Erica.   2. Authors, American—20th century—Biography.   I. Title.
PS3560.O56Z475   2006   2005055990
808'.5409—dc22

Printed in the United States of America
1   3   5   7   9   10   8   6   4   2

BOOK DESIGN BY AMANDA DEWEY

While the author has made every effort to provide accurate telephone numbers and
Internet addresses at the time of publication, neither the publisher nor the author
assumes any responsibility for errors, or for changes that occur after publication.
Further, the publisher does not have any control over and does not assume any responsibility for author or third-party web sites or their content.

CREDITS AND PERMISSIONS

ACKNOWLEDGMENTS

Portions of this book first appeared in *The New York Times Book Review* and *The Writer*. Deepest thanks to Ken Siman, who knows why.

To the memory of my father,

Seymour,

and

for Ken,

my cockeyed optimist

CONTENTS

When I was little, my ambition was to grow up to be a book. Not a writer. People can be killed like ants. Writers are not hard to kill either. But not books. However systematically you try to destroy them, there is always a chance that a copy will survive and continue to enjoy a shelf-life in some corner of an out-of-the-way library somewhere, in Reykjavik, Valladolid, or Vancouver.

AMOS OZ

James Baldwin, Allen Ginsberg, Erica Jong in 1978

INTRODUCTION

I started this as a book of advice to fledgling writers. Why? Probably because I was terrified of writing my next novel. I have been working on what I call, in my notebooks, "novel number nine" for more years than I want to admit. I start it, write two hundred or so pages and let myself be tempted into another project—a novel about Sappho in ancient Greece, a memoir about my life as a writer, anything that will distract me from the novel bubbling in my brain.

After many false starts, I finally know this novel has

to be about Isadora Wing as a woman of a certain age. That fills me with fear of writing. Going back to my most famous heroine after the ravages of time have chastened us both cannot be a painless proposition. Isadora has baggage and so does her author. It may be Goyard or Vuitton baggage, but it's baggage nonetheless. And despite what my loyal readers may think, I have never found it easy to reveal myself on the page.

I wrote my first novel, *Fear of Flying*, telling myself no one would ever read it. I wrote my other novels that way too—though the pretense was harder to achieve. My historical novels were the most pleasurable to write because I could retreat to eighteenth-century England or sixteenth-century Venice or ancient Greece. Wearing a mask is fun. Behind a mask, as Venetian revelers knew, you feel free.

When *Fear of Flying* sold an obscene number of copies and was read all over the world—thankfully, it continues to be read—I had to learn to draw back and find privacy for the next foray. Success can be as daunting as failure. I felt public—like a frog (with apologies to Emily Dickinson). Everyone judged me against a debut I made when I was young and green. Everyone constantly referred to "that book."

It's a universal fantasy to have a book that becomes a

phenomenon and is read—or perhaps skimmed—even by people who don't usually read. Some of them have strong opinions about the book without having ever cracked the spine. But beyond that early, unlikely coup, I wanted to have a shelf of books after my name. I didn't want to be a flash in the pan. My poetry and my historical novels kept me challenging myself even if the rest of the world only wanted *Fear of Flying* over and over again. Besides, as a defrocked academic, I loved holing up in a library and doing research. It was certainly more soothing than trying to live up to Erica "Zipless Fuck" Jong.

I'm not disowning my first novel. I'm proud of it. I think it has guts and juice—two things I prize. But I wrote it when I was very young—more than three and half decades ago.

So I spent five years evading my next novel and found solace in a book of advice to young writers I had in my computer. I had also been making notes for *it* for fifteen years! (My books tend to gestate like baby elephants.) I kept a little blue Chinese silk notebook full of advice from the great and the near great—as Mel Brooks and Carl Reiner's 2000 Year Old Man would say. I published some of it on my web site, some in *The New York Times Book Review*—a long piece about how Sylvia Plath had influenced my generation of writers—and some in

The Writer. Aspiring writers wrote to tell me my thoughts on writing were helpful. The first draft of the writing book contained such things as this list:

TWENTY-ONE RULES FOR WRITERS

1. Have faith—not cynicism.
2. Dare to dream.
3. Take your mind off publication.
4. Write for joy.
5. Get the reader to turn the page.
6. Forget politics (let your real politics shine through).
7. Forget intellect.
8. Forget ego.
9. Be a beginner.
10. Accept change.
11. Don't think your mind needs altering.
12. Don't expect approval for telling the truth.
13. Use everything.
14. Remember that writing is dangerous if it's any good.
15. Let sex (the body, the physical world) in!
16. Forget critics.
17. Tell your truth, not the world's.

18. Remember to be earthbound.
19. Remember to be wild!
20. Write for the child (in yourself and others).
21. There are no rules.

Actually this was all advice to *myself* when I was petrified about putting one word on the page. I could have published this self-help book if I chose to. I had a publisher who wanted it, paid for it and scheduled it. But the more I looked at it, the more dismayed I became.

There were too damn many books on writing! We needed more *readers,* not more writers. We had a whole industry of writing workshops. I myself went to guest lecture at them and found myself encouraging people who would *never* be writers, who hadn't the guts to be honest or hadn't the talent for words or hadn't the *zitzfleisch.* They were good kids or earnest adults and I had the social worker's instinct to help the needy. And I was paid those lecture fees to tide me over to the next book. Sometimes I even did it for free if a good friend or my daughter asked me. I love teaching; it was my first and only real job.

But writing is a god-awful profession. One year you get an advance and two years later you've spent it and the book is nowhere near finished. Most writers can't make a living without teaching or editing or working in advertising or journalism or TV or writing movies that never get made.

Why was I recommending this purgatory to people? Only if you have *no other choice* should you be a writer. Publishers are getting leaner and meaner. Advances are going down and you're only as good as your last sales figures. Even agents don't want you if you've had a flop. Literary writers used to regularly make the best-seller list when I started. Now romance novels that were once luridly paperbacked in drugstores—or novels by committees using a brand name—mostly monopolize the list.

Not that I have a problem with syndicate-written books, if they announce their syndicate on the cover. Anything that gets people reading is good. The Nancy Drew mysteries were written by committee and I adored Nancy Drew when I was eight, nine and ten. Summers on Fire Island, I used to save my wagoning and babysitting money to buy the latest Nancy Drew and read it through in two hours. I loved boyfriend Ned Nickerson and Nancy's red "roadster" and her "tomboy" friend George. I'm sorry they ever updated the series. It was both quaint and true—the perfect story of a motherless girl who loved her daddy. I felt it was the story of my life.

In contrast, my daughter, Molly, spent her whole childhood saying, "I'll never be a writer! I don't know why *anyone* would be! The first year we go to Europe and by the third year we're totally broke and you're hysterical and looking for teaching jobs." Then she turned nineteen and sat down and wrote *Normal Girl*. Clearly, she had no choice. She published it at twenty-one and immediately wrote *Girl Maladjusted*—a book of satirical essays she published at twenty-six when she had a year-old baby. She was driven—just like her mother. She had no choice but to write. And she refused to let me help her. She found her own agent and her own publisher. Without that drivenness—and a trust fund or Grandpa paying the bills—who can write? Only people who can live in cold-water flats and like it.

So why was I going into the advice business? My job was to tell the truth as I saw it. I had always been a shit disturber. And I had never received unequivocal praise. In fact I had been proud of being controversial. The brickbats told me I was doing something right.

So tell the truth, I told myself. That's your job, not advice and self-help.

And then I had a pivotal experience. Invited to speak at graduation for the College of Staten Island of the City University of New York (and be awarded my first honorary doctorate), I decided to tell the students the truth instead of mouthing hollow words of encouragement. I knew that Staten Island was a red borough in an otherwise blue city. I knew that my audience was likely to be composed of the sons and daughters of firefighters and cops who voted for George W. Bush. But what was the point of being chosen as commencement speaker if I was just going to soothe them and tell them what they wanted to hear?

What would *I* have wanted to hear at age twenty-one? What would my favorite authors—Jonathan Swift, Isaac Bashevis Singer, Pablo Neruda, Walt Whitman or Emily Dickinson—have talked about? They certainly wouldn't say "Seize the day or be seized by it" or "Write your dream on an egg and watch it hatch" or "Follow your bliss"—which may have been fresh when Joseph Campbell first said it to Bill Moyers but was now tattered and shopworn from all the New Agers who had tried it on and paraded about in it.

There was only one way to tell the truth. And that was to tell the kids and their parents and professors why I was there. I was there because I was a writer and a writer is someone who takes the universal whore of language and turns her into a virgin again. I wasn't going to coast on clichés. I was going to talk about the power of words—something I had been thinking a great deal about since the so-called war on terror dragged on and on, kidnapping the language and proliferating terrorists. Language, I thought, has never been more abused. And here's what I said:

> *Language matters because whoever controls the words controls the conversation, because whoever controls the conversation controls its outcome, because whoever frames the debate has already won it, because telling the truth has become harder and harder to achieve in an America drowning in Orwellian Newspeak.*
>
> *Telling the truth has never been easy—not for Jonathan Swift or Alexander Pope or Thomas Paine or Thomas Jefferson. Not for Mary Wollstonecraft—or any Enlightenment scribe. But now the Anglo-American idiom has been captured by deliberate liars: politicians, movie stars, advertisers and the corporations they write for, New Age gurus and other celebrities who all have what they think are good reasons to say the opposite of what they mean.*
>
> *The Misleader-in-Chief says "healthy forests" when he means clear-cutting trees, "clear skies" when he means pollution. His generals say "pacify"*

when they mean killing people, "collateral damage" when they mean killing foreign civilians. They say "friendly fire" when they mean killing our own soldiers. And it's not only our government that's deliberately lying to us.

Movie stars tell us that they're in love when they're just doing PR—think of Tom Cruise and Katie Holmes. Most people think their love is loveless, but they've pledged it on Oprah so it must be true. Did Oprah believe them? I doubt it. She's smart.

New Age gurus may be the worst word corrupters of all. Do we really need "wellness" when we have health? Do we need "healers" rather than physicians? (The words mean the same thing, but one sounds more "alternative"—another cant word.) Do we need "holistic" when we have "whole"? Is holistic somehow cooler than whole? It certainly has more syllables. Simplicity of language can contain the most profound ideas, as Jonathan Swift taught us. Wellness is not better than health. It only sounds fancier.

Not long ago I read on a "wellness web site" that chocolate is good for your heart—but not when it is mixed with fat and sugar and made into candy bars. This has not stopped the Mars company from claim-

ing the heart-healthy effects of their chocolates. "Heart-healthy," by the way, is another phrase that sounds like a great deal more than it is.

You cannot tell the truth when words are corrupted. Our country was founded on the notion that the plain words of the people are more important than the fancy words of kings. We admire George Washington not only for refusing to be king but also for not sanctioning lying—even though the cherry-tree story may be wholly apocryphal. We hold politicians to a much lesser standard today. We expect them to lie to us. We grant them the latitude to lie. We are lax about holding them to their word. We don't expect them to tell the truth about power any more than we expect movie stars to tell the truth about love. And we write off many lies as PR. Having stopped expecting truth, we rarely get it.

I've never stopped expecting it, never stopped trying my best to tell it and never stopped getting mad when it is not told to me. Why do I care so much? God only knows. I was born that way. I've made it my mission in writing to get other people to hate lies too.

Why is getting mad at lies so important? Because our survival depends on it, our republic depends on

it. Our lives depend on it—whether it's pharmaceu-
tical companies lying about drugs or chemical cor-
porations lying about pollution or politicians lying
about why our young people are coming home in
flag-draped boxes. We are in danger unless we know
the truth, and the truth depends on words.

During the Vietnam War we used to say that
people came home in "body bags." Those words
became politicized, so now the military speaks of
"transfer tubes"—transferring "folks" (as the Presi-
dent says) from the battlefield to the cemetery, I
guess. This happens after "the patient failed to fulfill
his wellness potential"—i.e., died.

It was when I said this in my commencement speech
that the faculty and some students started to cheer and
others started to loudly boo while they passed various
beach balls above their heads through the crowd.

My speech had started very late because three un-
announced politicians had been limousined up to the
outdoor podium and wedged in front of the other
speakers—like the college president, the provost of City
University, the dean of the faculty, the winner of the top
student prize and me. The pols had been nowhere in evidence when the academic procession began at nine-

thirty in the morning. So we all sat there in our gowns and hoods and mortarboards while some nameless nerd who was hopelessly running for mayor of New York City, Senator Chuck Schumer and a hopeless would-be challenger to Senator Hillary Clinton talked on and on about their own triumphs.

Chuck Schumer was mercifully brief. He told the audience that he was the one they should thank for the deductibility of college tuition. I wistfully remembered those days in the sixties when I taught at CCNY and tuition was free. This generation of students probably didn't even know about the great ideal of college education for all who were capable. They worked two or three jobs and incurred enormous tuition debts (or their parents did) and yet they kept voting for a President who thought only the rich should have college degrees. Their ignorance of history pained me. I am becoming an old fart, I thought, woolgathering about free college tuition at CUNY. Young people just assume they have no choice but to begin their adult lives deep in debt. Surely they would shoot the messenger if I talked about the antique ideal of free education. I decided I would keep my speech about language and telling the truth but cut it as short as I could.

Orwellian Newspeak is everywhere in the air, I said.

Senator Orrin Hatch has alleged "capital punishment is our society's recognition of the sanctity of human life." I could go on and on. There is no dearth of examples.

Why would someone like me spend her whole life indoors playing with words? Because words often determine who wins or who loses. When the anti-choice movement coined "pro-life," it was just a matter of time before they won the debate. "Pro-life" was a brilliant if misleading choice—pun intended. I think it's entirely possible that we will have to lose choice to get it back again. Nobody can get behind the right to abortion now that the sonogram lets us see all the little fingers and toes. It used to be the moment you first heard the heartbeat that melted your maternal or paternal heart. Now it's the first sonogram. Young parents-to-be show the first sonogram to their parents and everyone weeps. How can they not? Life is beginning again. How can one be unmoved?

I have spent my life and my lucre supporting *Roe v. Wade*, yet now I understand the so-called pro-life activists. I hardly agree with them, but I do understand them. Roe, schmo. Privacy is an abstract concept compared to those little fingers and toes. We old lefty liberals didn't know what hit us when the sonogram was invented. And "pro-life" is so much sexier than "pro-choice." Never mind that many pro-lifers love the death penalty, they have the better slogan and we are stuck with the vagueness of "choice."

So language matters. It matters a lot. If it's not clear, the motivations aren't either. Murky language means somebody wants to pick your pocket. Phrases like "wellness web site" and "heart-healthy" mean that your credit card will soon be punched. Phrases like "axis of evil" and "9/11 changed everything" mean that your draft card may be the next thing punched. And locutions like "the bravest that fell" and "honor the fallen" mean that you may soon be among them. All these phrases are meant to keep you from thinking. All these slogans are meant to instill those fuzzy feelings of pride and patriotism that prevent clear thinking.

Hell—I have felt these fuzzy, patriotic stirrings myself. After 9/11, I dreamed of joining the CIA! Not that the CIA would have taken a woman with a reputation for writing about the Zipless Fuck! But I was full of fervor to help my country. I wandered around my native city in a daze, trying to think of ways I could protect New York from future terrorist attacks.

I can be moved by fuzzy false patriotism just like anyone else. But sooner or later I try to wake myself up.

Here the cheers from the faculty and students got louder and the boos of the parents increased. They didn't want me in the CIA (or CIA, as insiders call it). They probably wanted me in Guantánamo or Abu Ghraib.

Why should anyone want to keep you from thinking? There are only a couple of possibilities: to pick your pocket, to cover up something or to put your life at risk while pretending to protect you.

If Newspeak narrows the range of thought, then clear speaking expands it again. If New Age cant obfuscates truth with fancy verbiage, then puncturing it shows us the hollowness at its core. If political speech is meant to lull you into unconsciousness with ready-made slogans, then clear speech wakes you up.

The labels "right" and "left" are inadequate to explain what people care about, I think. They have become new means of censorship and obfuscation. We shut out truth by saying "right" and "left." Nobody really thinks of herself as right or left. She thinks of herself as a person with complex views.

We face the greatest danger today from orthodoxies with their automatic assumptions. And since the politicians, journalists, advertisers and New Age gurus divide us into right and left, we are lulled into doing it ourselves even though we know our views cannot be neatly bracketed that way. That way leads to foggy thinking and having our pockets picked.

I finished my speech to cheers and "bravas" as well as hisses and boos. Good, I thought to myself, if I'm getting this reaction, I must be doing something right.

I spent the afternoon meeting the English Department and attending their special small ceremony and celebrating the graduates and faculty at the home of the president of CSI. Most of the students and faculty I met were energized by my speech. They were glad it had not been standard-issue platitudes.

The next day the local papers reported that I was

both cheered and booed—but stressed the booing. It was as if I'd been set up. My web site contained both reactions—"you commie, kike bitch" and "thank God you told the truth."

My books had always gotten both hate mail and huzzas. I was used to it. What use is a writer if she doesn't rile people up? What use is a teacher if he isn't made to drink hemlock in the end? In the olden days they threw writers into oubliettes and eventually condemned them to death. Witches—any women who questioned the status quo—were burned at the stake. How could I complain about a few boos? Boos were honors. They meant I was questioning authority, speaking truth to power. They meant I was trying to tell the truth—my quixotic calling.

So here I am, writing for my life: telling how I published two well-received volumes of poetry in my twenties and then went all to hell with a scandalous first novel that I didn't even think was scandalous when I was writing it.

Telling how "that book" went on and on and on so it almost obliterated everything else I did; how I became a mother (once), a stepmother (once), a grandmother (twice so far) and a wife (four times) and still went on trying to tell the truth as I saw it. I'm not planning to cover up all my stumbles along the way nor my many mistakes nor all the times I made an absolute fool of myself.

Writing a book in your twenties that becomes a worldwide phenomenon hardly prepares you for the silence and despair of a writer's life. My life was not typical. But no writer's life is typical. By its very nature, writing is unique to every writer. Practicing writing is like practicing freedom. You are always on your way, never there. People are constantly asking, "How did you do it?" After a while you start to ask yourself. This book is an attempt to answer that question—regrets, mistakes, divorces, lawsuits and all.

I.

SLEEPING *with* DEMONS, *or* SEDUCTION

I loved the entanglings of genitals,
And out of blood and love, I carved my poems.

PABLO NERUDA

Isaac Bashevis Singer wrote a wonderful story called "Taibele and Her Demon." In it, a man pretending to be a demon visits by night a pretty young woman whose children have died and whose husband has walked out in utter despair.

At first the demon terrifies her with his ugliness, but then she falls in love with him—as much for his vivid stories of hell and heaven as for his demonic lovemaking. She completely forgets that he's ugly and becomes more and more attached to him—even though after a while she can see his human failings. Yes, this demon "perspired, sneezed, hiccupped, yawned." Yes, "sometimes his breath smelled of onion, sometimes of garlic. . . . His body felt like the body of her husband, bony and hairy, with an Adam's apple and a navel. . . . His feet were not goose feet, but human with nails and frost blisters.

"Once Taibele asked him the meaning of these things, and Hurmizah [the demon's assumed name] explained: 'When one of us consorts with a human female, he assumes the shape of a man. Otherwise she would die of fright.'

"Yes, Taibele got used to him and loved him. She was no longer terrified of him and his impish antics."

Perhaps she suspected he was really a man, but not wanting to know it, she refused to. Singer's story is a kind of reverse Scheherazade: the woman falls in love with the teller of tales and welcomes his lovemaking no matter what his looks. But it is more than that. It's a fable of disguise between a woman and a man, who *both* need the disguise to give each other permission to love each other. She needs to believe he is a demon so that she thinks she has no choice but to submit to him. He needs to be convinced that she believes him in order to keep up the elaborate fantasy that turns her on. Many marriages are based on less.

The story of Taibele has always seemed to me the perfect metaphor for my life as a writer.

The job of the writer is to seduce the demons of creativity and make up stories. Often you go to bed with a man who claims to be a demon and later you find out he's just an everyday slob. By then he may have inspired a novel. The novel remains though the demon has departed.

I wrote to my friend Ken Follett about the metaphorical resonance I found in the Singer story. He read the story. Then, he asked me in an e-mail:

"Do you really see yourself as a woman who slept with someone who claimed to be the Devil, but then turned out to be an ordinary slob?"

He answered his own question:

"Let me guess. You're going to reply: 'Yes—every damn time.'"

"But once, the demon was not unmasked."

"When was that?" my friend asked.

"I will tell you by and by."

Taibele doesn't want to acknowledge that her lover is merely human. She needs the belief in demons to complete her sexual life. She needs to believe in demons because otherwise she'd be betraying her wandering husband. And she is not that kind of girl.

The best stories don't have one metaphor but are layered with many. Isaac Bashevis Singer was too thoughtful a writer to give us a single metaphor. He gives us so many that the tale resonates endlessly—the definition of a great story.

So who is *my* demon?

He is wild, uncivilized and lives entirely in the moment. He makes up stories and acts them out. He is never polite. He didn't go to college and certainly did not get an MFA at Iowa. He doesn't know which fork to use. He never heard about the Ten Commandments— and certainly not the one about adultery. He has hairy feet and very likely a tail.

Let's see if you can tell when the demon appears. It shouldn't be hard. He casts a jagged shadow. And he leaves a wet spot on the sheet.

Of course, for male writers he is a she. She becomes whatever physical type the writer favors, since men care so much more about appearance than women do. Does he like big tits with rosy nipples? She has them. Does he like steatopygous asses? She has one that resembles twin planets. Does he like blue eyes? She has them. Brown? They've just changed color. Is he a chubby chaser? She's chubby too. Is he a modelizer? (ugh—what a stupid word)—then she's skinny. At six-foot-four with slanty Slavic cheekbones, green eyes with neon yellow pupils, she weighs in at ninety-nine pounds. In life, she reminds you of Auschwitz. In bed, she feels like a bicycle. But in photos she looks like a goddess.

For a gay writer, he's the perfect boy. He has idealized muscles like Michelangelo's *David*. He may even be a lovely Bacchus or a Hermes with winged sandals.

He's Greek, of course. The Greeks had the most beautiful boys. And they competed naked with their adorable cocks bound up in leather thongs so as not to swing. Oh what rapture to watch them run! Nobody was gay or straight then—only human.

I always knew I was a writer and that writing would define my life. How I knew this I can't say, but when I was seven, I used to kiss the pictures of writers on the backs of books. If I had known what I now know of writers, would I have done that? Probably not. "Let me kiss the hand that wrote *Ulysses*," some abject fan once asked James Joyce. "You don't know where else it's been," he countered.

I knew I loved writers. I vividly remember being a

child in the big room on Seventy-seventh Street (facing south over the water tanks of the Upper West Side and lighted by the moon and the General Motors sign). I shared that room with both my sisters. Coming in to kiss us goodnight, my mother saw me kissing the picture of Louisa May Alcott on the back of *Little Women* and observed ironically, "She's dead." Probably she was jealous that I loved someone other than her. My mother's fierce, envious love left no room for other women mentors. But her throwaway comment made writing seem even more miraculous: the dead could still communicate. I adored writers because even from the grave they were able to take me away on magical voyages.

The books I treasured as a child—the Oz books, *At the Back of the North Wind, Gulliver's Travels*—were all about such voyages. And not surprisingly, the form I revert to again and again is a picaresque in which a lucky naïf encounters all sorts of baddies but nevertheless makes it alive to the happy ending. I never plan this plot, but its template must be embedded in my unconscious. I write such books, I guess, because I cherished such stories when I was young. And I write always in the hopes of being transported to some enchanted place. I need the process of writing to keep from going mad.

Or perhaps it was all Oedipal—a way of seducing my father by becoming famous. Fame was a thing he prized. If I became famous, he would love me best of the three sisters. Perhaps it was as simple—and complex—as that.

If I were a child today, would I be equally in love with books? My daughter was a television watcher who came late to books but is now a convert. And my grandson is already book-obsessed. At not yet two, he shouts "Read! Read!" and hands me an unruly stack of books. Perhaps the reading addiction cannot be suppressed. I hope not. We live in a world so full of willful distractions that it seems unlikely that pursuits as solitary as writing and reading can survive. In airports, gyms, banks, diners, manicure parlors, TV news assaults you. On the telephone you are obliged to listen to music you would never choose. Cell-phone junkies (including me) tell you details of their dinners, dynastic complications and medical disorders you don't want to know. All your senses scream for serenity.

Perhaps, paradoxically, that is why writing has never been so important—despite the fact that fewer and fewer people have time to read. Writing and reading enable you to reclaim the inside of your skull. They erase the slate scribbled with distractions. For me it is a kind of meditation. I am never so calm as after I have written. And the next morning I will feel the familiar anxiety and I will have to begin the process all over again.

Henry Miller used to say that he wrote fifty pages before he could hear the book's "fetal heartbeat." Ernest Hemingway (that great overrated icon) used to look out at the rooftops of Paris and say to himself, "All you have to do is write one true sentence. Write the truest sentence that you know." "We make ourselves real by telling the truth," the poet-monk-philosopher Thomas Merton says. And that, for me, is the secret of writing.

At some point in my odyssey from young poet/ graduate student to scandalous first novelist, I met a man. I was always meeting men in those days. He was an elderly publisher with a long track record of publishing books that were initially banned, like Nabokov's *Lolita* and D. H. Lawrence's *Lady Chatterley's Lover.* He also published plenty of trash, as successful publishers must: books about UFOs, astrological predictions about the stock market and sexual how-tos.

Sexual how-tos never go out of style, but each age must invent its own. In my parents' era, sex books hid under white coats and stethoscopes; their authors were doctors, like Eustace Chesser, M.D., the author of *Love Without Fear,* a book I found in Japan on a paperback rack at Hakone, a ski resort at the foot of Mount Fuji. The resort was in a tiny town and I stalked that book, afraid to buy yet afraid not to buy. Finally I did buy it and escaped from my parents and younger sister to read it in the thermal baths underneath the hotel where the guests swam nude, enjoying the Japanese lack of shame about nakedness.

In my generation of war babies, Alex Comfort, *philosophe extraordinaire,* took over the sex-advice specialty in *The Joy of Sex* and *More Joy.* (Once, in the late seventies, I was offered a truckload of greenbacks to write *The Joy of Woman,* but I demurred, thinking it would permanently typecast me as a sex writer. I turned down the filthy lucre and got typecast anyway.)

The early seventies were all about the clitoris. The clitoris was queen. It was impossible to escape the seventies without climbing over the clitoris. Apparently, for centuries men had been unable to find it. And women were pissed. Then Masters and Johnson came along, stuck a transparent electric dildo filled with transistors into various cunts, videoed them and discovered that the clitoris was definitely the place where female orgasms began. So Freud was wrong! There *were* no vaginal orgasms! The clitoris was the It girl of the era.

If you had missed Masters and Johnson in their white coats (de rigueur for sexologists), you could read Shere Hite. She had interviewed three thousand women and discovered that "most women can orgasm easily during clitoral or pubic area stimulation but only one third can orgasm easily from the actual act, i.e., penetration." This was a big fuck-you to men, who apparently were so benighted they thought women could all come in thirty seconds from penetration by a hasty ejaculator.

Of course all through history there had been a few men (mostly in lovely Mediterranean countries that seem to glide on olive oil) who knew how to please a woman, but unless you moved to Italy at puberty there were apparently not enough to go around. Besides, you had to put up with their omnipotent mothers. So Hite's book caused a sensation. A few years later, it was supplanted by the G-spot, which everyone was determined to find whether they had one or not.

So back to the elderly publisher—whom I'll call Wagstaff, may he rest in peace. He had published many books about the triumphant clitoris. He said he loved my first two books of poetry, *Fruits & Vegetables* and *Half-*

Lives. He took me to the Rose Room at the Algonquin to see if I was writing a novel. I was.

We ordered jellied consommé and crab salad and too much wine. We were sitting side by side on a banquette and his mottled fingers crept toward my bare thighs. It was midsummer and the micro-miniskirt was in fashion. I moved away—which was not easy to do on the sticky banquettes of the Rose Room. The waiter came by and brought more wine. (Those were the days when publishing lunches were bibulous rather than ostentatiously abstemious.)

"So you're writing a novel?"

"About a psychiatrist's wife who takes off on a mad picaresque adventure with—"

"If it's anything like your poems, I'm your publisher."

"Well, maybe you should see it first."

"I don't need to see it. My gut tells me it's great. How do I get it?" His old eyes glittered like a lizard's. "I'll pay anything."

I thought of the biggest advance I could. I had read in *Publishers Weekly* that a first novelist got $500,000.

"Half a million," I said sheepishly. That would make my father proud—my father who had left show business to go into the tchotchke biz and always regretted it.

"Done," said the glittering lizard.

What had I said? I had an agent. I was not allowed to bargain with an old reptile at lunch.

"Best not to discuss money with me," I said, hastily backpedaling. What if I could get more? "Talk to Anita, my agent."

He licked his dry and crumbling lips. "I shall. All the best novelists started as poets," he said. "Hemingway wrote poems. James Joyce. Thomas Hardy. D. H. Lawrence. It all starts with metaphor. You know, my other passion is rare books."

"It is?" I adored rare books myself—even though I had never owned any (I had coveted them in the Rare Book Room at the Butler Library). To me they were the sexiest things in the world. Sexier than "The Diamond as Big as the Ritz"—that made F. Scott Fitzgerald's heart beat faster.

"I've just bought a very fine copy of Keats's *Endymion*. I would love to share it with you."

"Keats is my absolutely favorite poet."

"And I have a first of *Leaves of Grass* I'd love to show you too."

My heart was racing. My body was becoming electric. "I love *Leaves of Grass*."

"My office is just down the street," the old roué said. Now, this was not his *real* office in his publishing house. It was an additional little office he kept in the building *The New Yorker* was in, right down the block.

He led me there. We went up in the elevator as he rattled his keys. There, on a high floor, was an office that was more like a book depository (with all the associations that conveyed to someone of my generation). One room with a sooty window, a metal desk and book stacks like a public library. He went to these stacks and pulled out two volumes encased in what I now know are called "clamshells." Carefully, and with ceremony, he pulled *Endymion* from its clamshell and placed it before me on his desk.

A thing of beauty is a joy for ever:
Its loveliness increases; it will never
Pass into nothingness; but still will keep
A bower quiet for us, and a sleep . . .

I read this and remembered my college adoration of Keats, how I had visited his house in Hampstead when I was nineteen and written a poem about it, how I had gone on to visit the house where he died in Rome and written about that too. I was enchanted. I read on:

. . . in spite of all,
Some shape of beauty moves away the pall

From our dark spirits. Such the sun, the moon,
Trees old, and young, sprouting a shady boon
For simple sheep; and such are daffodils
With the green world they live in . . .

I was living in a green world even in that dusty room. I could have been that young Greek shepherd falling in love with Cynthia, the moon goddess.

Wagstaff then produced *Leaves of Grass* with its frontispiece of good gray Walt Whitman. He spread it out on his desk and flipped it open:

There was a child went forth every day;
And the first object he look'd upon, that object he
became;
And that object became part of him for the day, or a
certain part of the day, or for many years, or
stretching cycles of years.

The early lilacs became part of this child,
And grass, and white and red morning-glories, and
white and red clover, and the song of the phoebe-
bird,
. . . curiously below there—and the beautiful
curious liquid,

*And the water-plants with their graceful flat
heads—all became part of him.*

So I became part of the book. Its creamy pages
became my flesh and its greenness entered my heart and
before I knew it, the mottled old publisher was embracing me from behind and then turning me around to
kiss his wrinkled lips. Somehow, in unison with Walt
Whitman, who became everything he looked upon, who
merged with the people on the street who caught his
empathic gaze, I was on my knees before the elderly publisher. Then somehow I was sucking his flabby prick
(how did it get to my mouth?) for every atom of him as
well belonged to me.

It took him forever to come. He was old and the sap
was congealed. It wasn't running. It was limping. It was
creeping. But the social worker in me felt sorry for his
age and his avid desire, so I persevered. (Besides, once
you're on your knees it's tough to escape gracefully.)
Visions of rare books in my library sustained me. What
madness was going through my addled brain? Surely he
would give me a first edition—or two—in exchange for
this arduous blow job? It went on and on. This was the
era of *Deep Throat,* but I can assure you my clitoris was
not anywhere in the vicinity of my tonsils. He would lose

his erection, and then torturedly get it back. If I had been looking at a clock, it would surely have been going backwards. But I was looking at those first editions, which had turned me on in the first place. Finally, he came, dribblingly—and full of apologetic palaver.

"What can I do for *you*?" he asked. "A first edition or two would be nice," the gold-digger girl I never was would have said.

"Is it true that Keats died a virgin?" I asked, getting up, without replying to his offer. I couldn't bear for him to touch me. It was Keats I wanted.

"Sad if he did. So sad. What a waste of poetry!" the elderly publisher said. Did he think of poetry only as a means of seduction? Well, it worked, didn't it?

The next day a large brown package arrived at my house on Seventy-seventh Street.

It was so carefully wrapped, it *must* be a first edition. First there was this note:

"I cannot thank you enough for your bravado, your intelligence, your sheer joyousness. You are a true Whitmanic spirit."

So I unwrapped and unwrapped and unwrapped, dreaming of first editions. There within the bubble wrap and plastic and brown paper was a facsimile 1855 edition of *Leaves of Grass*.

I felt as if I'd been betrayed. *I didn't give him a facsimile blow job!* What's more, he totally forgot about the pricey advance.

So I broke my own rule: Never get sexually involved with a publisher. I was to break it once more, to my consternation. And I was to make a most inconvenient enemy in Martha Stewart. But that was much later, when I had already published three novels and five books of poetry. First, I need to continue with the lives of the poets.

I met Ted Hughes around the same time I met the elderly publisher—early seventies. He had just published his deathward poem cycle called *Crow: From the Life and Songs of the Crow.* In these astonishing poems, a crow with a bloody beak sits in a tree looking down on a world in love with death. The poems were gory and fierce, full of nature red in tooth and claw—not surprising for a poet whose two lovers had committed suicide, the second taking their child along.

The reasons were different for each—if suicide can ever have a reason. Assia Wevill, whom Ted Hughes apparently fell for while he was still with Sylvia Plath, was the child of Holocaust survivors—a group at great risk for suicide. Sylvia Plath had suffered depressions and suicide attempts during her adolescence, as she recounted in her novel, *The Bell Jar*. Both women were in love with Ted Hughes—who cannot have been an easy man to love but was compelling. When I met him, I understood why both these brilliant women fell.

He was fiercely sexy, with a vampirish, warlock appeal. He hulked. He was tall and his shoulders were broad. His hair fell against his broad forehead. He had a square jaw and an intense gaze and he reeked of virility. Moreover, he knew how irresistible he was in the Heathcliff fashion, and he did the wildman-from-the-moors thing on me full force when we met. He was a born seducer and only my terror of Sylvia's ghost kept me from being seduced.

I remember sitting across a bar table with Ted and his friend Luke while Ted put the poetic moves on me. Knowing I'd want an autographed book, he snatched my copy of *Crow* and drew, on the title page, a lecherous snake climbing an Edenic tree. "To Erica, a beautiful Surprise," he scribbled flirtatiously, as he must have done with every woman he met. You could inhale the man's pheromones across the table—this stink of masculinity and musk that must have worked on countless girls. His eyes held you in his gaze as if you were the only person on the planet. The only other man I've met who had such intensity was Ingmar Bergman, another born seducer—in the gloomy northern style. Are these men from the cold and gloomy north so sexy because they taunt you with the promise of sex that can melt icebergs? Or is it the intensity of genius that attracts? Genius is a strong aphrodisiac.

I have treasured Ted's inscription for years and wished we had fucked. But Hughes's flirtations were legendary. Since his death, from cancer in 1998, dozens of women have come forward to claim that he was their secret lover. Perhaps I was lucky the flirtation was never consummated. At least that way I could keep him as my secret demon.

"In lapidary inscriptions, a man is not upon oath," Samuel Johnson wrote. Nor in book inscriptions, I would add, especially those penned after the adrenaline rush of reading one's poems to adoring female fans. My temperature rose and with it my panic. I taxied home to my husband on the West Side, my head full of the hottest fantasies. Of course we fucked our brains out with me imagining Ted.

I had become friends with an old friend of Sylvia Plath and Ted Hughes who'd brought me to Ted's reading. His name was Luke and he'd been at school with them. He told me that on their first meeting at a Cambridge party, Sylvia and Ted disappeared into a room to "make out" (as we said in the fifties) and emerged several minutes later with Ted bleeding copiously from a bite Sylvia had given him on the cheek.

Sylvia Plath recounts the same tale in her journal (*The Journals of Sylvia Plath*, 1982).

> *Then the worst thing happened, that big, dark, hunky boy, the only one there huge enough for me, who had been hunching around over women, and whose name I had asked the minute I came in the room, but nobody told me, came over and was looking hard in my eyes and it was Ted Hughes. I started yelling again about his poems and quoting . . . and bang the door was shut and he was sloshing brandy into a glass and I was sloshing it at the place where my mouth was when I last knew about it.*
>
> *We shouted as if in a high wind, about the review, and he saying Dan knew I was beautiful . . . and then it came to the fact that I was all there, wasn't I, and I stamped and screamed yes . . . and he was stamping and he was stamping on the floor, and then he kissed me bang smash on the mouth and ripped my hair band off, my lovely red hairband*

*scarf which has weathered the sun and much love,
and whose like I shall never again find, and my
favorite silver earrings: hah, I shall keep, he barked.
And when he kissed my neck, I bit him long and hard
on the cheek, and when we came out of the room,
blood was running down his face . . . I can see how
women lie down for artists. The one man in the
room who was big as his poems, huge, with hulk and
dynamic chunks of words; his poems are strong and
blasting like a high wind in steel girders. And I
screamed in myself: oh to give myself crashing, fighting to you.*

This is practically Molly Bloom's soliloquy—but
with an overtone of masochism and violence—and if
there is a better description of seducing the demon, I
haven't found it—not even in Singer.

So Sylvia Plath seduced her demon, had two children
with him, and then he strayed and then she died, but the
simple causal relationship this implies is too pat, too
neat. Life is never neat.

Sylvia Plath redefined what it meant to be a woman
poet. No neurasthenic "toast-and-teasdale" (as Carolyn

Kizer called the women poets of the early twentieth century), but a full-blooded woman, seeking a full-blooded
man, and children—a life of creativity leavened by sex,
love, parenthood.

For those of us who grew up longing to be writers in
the fifties, there was no obvious female template. Creativity was portrayed as a mandrake root—male, with a
large gnarled phallus buried in the earth. Pull it out. Its
virility was unmistakable. Female writers didn't exist
on our critical radar or were cruelly mocked. Theodore
Roethke, a wonderful poet, complained of our tendency
"to stamp a tiny foot against God." Anatole Broyard, the
writer and critic, told my writing class at Barnard we
hadn't the sort of experiences that *made* writers. We
didn't get drunk at bars in Pigalle or pick up hookers in
seedy Left Bank hotels or run with the bulls in Pam-
plona. Our lives were too circumscribed. We didn't drink
enough. (Not yet, anyway.) We didn't puke in the street.
(Not yet, anyway.) We were "doomed" to be future mothers. Domesticated animals, future wives (many times over,
as it turned out), we didn't ride the painted bus with Neal
Cassady, or chant Blake with Ginsberg or even poach on
Barnard girls as Broyard did. We were too ladylike.

In college, we passionate future writers studied
Blake, Keats, and Byron, T. S. Eliot, Ezra Pound, Dylan

Thomas, W. H. Auden, Theodore Roethke, John Berry-
man, Robert Browning, etc. Yes, we knew there was a
Mrs. Browning, but hadn't she only written one treacly
poem—"How do I love thee? Let me count the ways"?
Emily Dickinson lurked in Butler Library in something
called the American Men of Letters series. Edna St. Vincent Millay, a Barnard graduate, whom we had pored
over as teenagers, was not on the Barnard syllabus.
Dorothy Parker, whom we also adored, was deemed a
light versifier, not worthy of academic interest. In fact,
the whole era of suffragists and flappers—our grandmothers' generation—occasionally surfaced as social
history, but mostly it was invisible, as was its message
that free women could change the world. Later we would
call that suffragist generation the First Wave of feminism
and ourselves the Second Wave. (Actually Mary Woll-
stonecraft was the First Wave, the suffragists the Second
and my generation the Third—but who's counting?)
Feminism, an Enlightenment ideal, is more honored in
the breach than in the observance—like free speech, the
brotherhood of man and the ideal of racial equality.
Feminism ebbs and flows like the sea. Yet the truth
remains that my contemporaries and I would have to
ride our own wave—whatever number we dubbed it—to
believe in ourselves as writers.

Here's who we did *not* read in college (in addition to Millay and Parker): Amy Lowell, Anna Wickham, Edith Sitwell, Stevie Smith, Louise Bogan, Ruth Pitter, Gertrude Stein, Laura Riding, Judith Wright, Gwendolyn Brooks, Kathleen Raine, Margaret Walker, Carolyn Kizer, Ruth Stone, Muriel Rukeyser, Elizabeth Bishop, Sara Teasdale, May Swenson, May Sarton, Grace Paley, Denise Levertov, Maxine Kumin, Anne Sexton—though all these women were published then. We do not like to admit that politics plays a part in literary reputations, but without politics we would still be invisible. Our daughters cannot even imagine female invisibility. We raised them telling them they could do anything and everything. We told them God might well be female. We told them we wanted them *because* they were girls. We filled their heads with female goddesses, women poets and women's history. (Dear Goddess, don't make me call it *herstory* or *womyns' history*—I may break out in hives.) The point is: We taught them to love themselves.

They are still condemned to the ghetto of chick lit, and reviewed poorly for writing about things women care about—proof of second-classness—but at least they are no longer silent.

When my daughter Molly started to write, it never occurred to her to write in a male persona. She knew she could be a writer. Her mother was a writer, her father was a writer and her grandfather was a writer. She did not doubt her right to a voice.

What a change we have wrought. When I see all these young women writing chick lit, I'm proud. They may be writing about sex and shopping and dumping Mr. Wrong for Mr. Right or Mr. Right for Mr. Wrong. They may have the white weddings and diamond rings we scorned as hopelessly bourgeois, but at least they're writing. They have their own voices and their voices are loud and insistent. We were afraid to stamp a tiny foot against God for fear that the guys would laugh. And laugh they did. Paul Theroux called Isadora Wing "a mammoth pudenda." Even intelligent writers were male chauvinist pigs in those days. Reviewing *Fear of Flying* in *The New Statesman,* Theroux must have had a full-scale panic attack. What else would explain his calling my heroine, and by extension her author, "a mammoth pudenda"? What was he afraid of? Obviously a huge *vagina dentata.* I hope he's gotten over that. I think I have, but I'm still bitching, so maybe not.

What would happen when women told their side of the story? Would the world split open? In a way, it *did.* And most of the results were sanguine. Fatherhood was liberated. Men can now admit they like being close to their kids. Women can admit they don't always. Life is less rigid. Women earn money. Men cook. Women say how much they hate housework. They are not ashamed to order out. They are not afraid of fantasy. They admit to having sexual dreams and feeling pure lust. They have sex with the occasional demon just for the fun of it. They have sex with their girlfriends and don't make a federal case out of it. Even the ones who want to stay home with their babies know they have choices.

I survived to have the last laugh. Keats notwithstanding, book reviews can't kill. Many of the men and women who were terrified by *Fear of Flying* have either gone silent or convinced themselves they always loved the book.

Now the girls of my daughter's generation have size-twelve feet and booming voices. They all have Black-Berries and Treos. They text-message their funky desires to their lovers. They read my books and think: *Why did my mother hide this from me? It's not that raunchy at all.*

We conveniently forget that Sylvia Plath was not-known until 1963, when she was already dead. Her entire public career was posthumous. Had she lived, would her poems have the same appeal? Or was the bloody fingerprint on the page part of the allure? An unanswerable question. We want to know that great poems have great consequences—both for their authors and readers.

When I was at Barnard, my writing teacher, the poet Robert Pack, used to talk about our response to works of art with this parable: "Suppose you see a canvas with a red slash across it and nothing more. You look at it and wonder what you think of it. Then suppose someone tells you that the artist cut off his right hand and made that crimson gash—does it change your view?"

In *The New Yorker* magazine of August 3, 1963, a remarkable sequence of poems appeared. They were by a poet whose name was not yet familiar to readers but whose voice sounded like no other. Under these poems was the intriguing attribution: Sylvia Plath (1932–1963). Since there was no Contributors section in Mr. Shawn's *New Yorker,* readers had no idea who the author of these astonishing poems might be. Her name was followed by the ominous double dates confirming that the author was no longer on this sad planet. She had gone, like Alcestis, to the Land of the Dead.

The sequence began with "Two Campers In Cloud Country" and ended with "The Moon and the Yew Tree."

This is the light of the mind, cold and planetary
The trees of the mind are black. The light is blue.
The grasses unload their griefs on my feet as if I
    were God . . .
I simply cannot see where there is to get to.

No one reading these poems could doubt that their author was more than "half in love with easeful death," as Keats had it. But then young poets are always in love with death and in love with love. This one was only thirty when she died.

I have fallen a long way. Clouds are flowering
Blue and mystical over the face of the stars
Inside the church, the saints will all be blue,
Floating on their delicate feet over the cold pews,
Their hands and faces stiff with holiness.
The moon sees nothing of this. She is bald and wild.
And the message of the yew tree is blackness—
    blackness and silence.

The impact these poems had is almost unimaginable now. In 1963, we still had a literary culture. *Reading* poems to oneself was not as rare as it is today (despite all the poetry slams and hip-hop jams). To young women who wrote poetry, these poems were galvanizing. Sylvia, whoever she was, had a fully evolved voice. Not wry and reeking of the bittersweet twenties like Dorothy Parker's or romantic/ironic/transcendentalist like Edna St. Vincent Millay's. Perhaps some of its confessional candor was nudged by Robert Lowell. Perhaps Anne Sexton had contributed something of her own dark menstrual madness. Nor was the voice influenced by the hymnal rhythms of Emily Dickinson's meditations on death and love. It was incomparable.

The poems were hypnotic—as Robert Lowell, her sometime teacher, later said in his introduction to *Ariel* (which appeared in 1965 in England, 1966 in America). They were unapologetically female. An Amazon wrote them riding bareback. She had cut off one breast and dipped her quill in her blood. We would never know precisely why she killed herself. Nor could we ask.

Why did she die? Who was responsible? How could she have left these driven, hurtling lines and, as we later learned, two helpless children? What did her husband, the rugged, seemingly heartless poet Ted Hughes, have to do with it? (Of course I never dared to ask him when we met.) He was her widower, executor, the father of Frieda and Nicholas (to whom her second book, when it appeared under the title *Ariel,* was dedicated).

We like our poets better when they're dead—especially our women poets. Sylvia knew this. She knew a lot about the suppression of women poets in the Age of Eliot and she was determined to overcome it—whatever the cost.

After three decades of fearless female writing, it's hard to credit how male-dominated the literary world was then. For my generation (which graduated from college in the midsixties, before they became "The Sixties"), poetry was a men's club. Sylvia Plath definitively broke open the territory to women. She made it possible to strip the female mind naked in print.

Anne Sexton had begun this journey with *To Bedlam and Part Way Back* in 1960. Sylvia Plath's extraordinary voice took us further. These two poets embodied the first surge of the Second Wave. Not surprisingly, poetry, which comes blood-warm straight out of the unconscious, led the way.

Of course I don't mean to imply that there were no earlier women poets who broke ground. Louise Bogan, Elizabeth Bishop, Gwendolyn Brooks, Denise Levertov, Marianne Moore, Ruth Stone, Muriel Rukeyser, Judith Wright, May Sarton, Carolyn Kizer and Adrienne Rich had all published extraordinary poems. And Marge Piercy, Margaret Atwood, Diane Wakoski, Joyce Carol

Oates and others were beginning to appear in the sixties. But perhaps it was the flamboyance of Plath's and Sexton's suicides that thrust their work into the larger public consciousness. Poetry was so important you would *die* for it. And in those days you had to. The gentlemen's club of poetry in the early sixties is well evoked by Carolyn Kizer's "Pro Femina," a poem I went back to again and again for courage:

> *I will speak about women of letters, for I'm in the*
>   *racket.*
> *Our biggest successes to date? Old maids to a woman.*
> *And our saddest conspicuous failures? The married*
>   *spinsters*
> *On loan to the husbands they treated like surrogate*
>   *fathers . . .*
> *Or the sad sonneteers, toast-and-teasdales we loved*
>   *at thirteen;*
> *Middle-aged virgins seducing the puerile anthologists*
> *Through lust-of-the-mind; barbiturate-drenched*
>   *Camilles*
> *With continuous periods, murmuring softly on*
>   *sofas*
> *When poetry wasn't a craft but a sickly effluvium,*

The air thick with incense, musk, and emotional
blackmail.

Kizer perfectly analyzed the problem of a craft in which the practitioners were all suicides and spinsters, even if they were married (a problem I have with the myth of Woolf—who often seems to be worshipped for her sexless married spinsterhood).

"From Sappho to myself, consider the fate of women," Kizer writes. "How unwomanly to discuss it!"

. . . we are the custodians of the world's best-kept
secret:
Merely the private lives of one-half of humanity.

Kizer was our diagnostician, but Plath and Sexton provided the cure. No apologies. No analyses. No tea and sympathy. Instead, we heard a voice speaking straight from the female gut. Though death-bound, Plath's voice was already exultant. "Hardly a woman at all, certainly not another 'poetess' but one of those . . . great classical heroines," Robert Lowell wrote. "These poems are playing Russian roulette with six cartridges in the cylinder." We had found our sixties Sappho—just after she leapt from the Leucadian cliff.

. . .

Now the brilliant, bipolar Lowell is dead and so is the fierce, sexy Ted Hughes. Now the children he raised are grown. Frieda is a painter and poet who somehow survived her childhood. She gets to tell her mother's tale, as is only right. The edition of *Ariel* published by her father was not identical to the manuscript her mother left, so at her publisher's suggestion Frieda Hughes resurrected that manuscript, even giving us facsimiles of the poems in typed and handwritten form (*Ariel: The Restored Edition*, 2004). We immediately see that Plath nearly called her second collection *Daddy and Other Poems* instead of *Ariel*. We feel Frieda Hughes's restraint in trying to be fair to both parents yet tell the truth as she sees it. "My father had a profound respect for my mother's work in spite of being one of the subjects of its fury," she writes.

The reticence of the dutiful daughter (Frieda is in her midforties) trying to make sense of her family history is riveting. Frieda is still trying to bring her parents back together again; all children of ruptured love stories want to. She speaks of the distortion of Plath's character and work by strangers, and in her stunning self-control you feel her pain. "The collection of the *Ariel* poems became symbolic to me of this possession of my mother and of the wider vilification of my father," she calmly says.

The reference, clearly, is to self-appointed defenders of Sylvia Plath who never knew her or Hughes, perhaps never even read their work. Plath's gravestone in Yorkshire was often defaced to obliterate "Hughes." What a child named Hughes might make of this we can only guess. "Criticism of my father was even leveled at his ownership of my mother's copyright, which fell to him on her death and which he used to directly benefit my brother and me," Frieda notes. "My father's editing of *Ariel* was seen to 'interfere' with the sanctity of my mother's suicide, as if, like some deity, everything associated with her must be enshrined and preserved as miraculous. . . . I did not want my mother's death to be commemorated as if it had won an award. I wanted her life to be celebrated."

I once took the brunt of the Plath industry's assault myself. Talking about her poetry and suicide at the Poetry Center of the 92nd Street Y in 1971, I was picketed by an angry posse because I refused to mouth the feminist orthodoxy of the time, that Hughes had *murdered* Plath. That Plath had a history of breakdowns in her college years was of no interest. My hecklers wanted to believe that a cruel husband done 'er in, whatever the "facts."

And the facts were hard to come by. Ted Hughes was shellshocked himself, and wanted to hide. He was also in love with the poet Assia Wevill, who committed suicide in 1969; their daughter also died by her mother's hand. Her suicide is often thought of as a copycat act (indeed, the method was the same). Reading about Plath and Hughes, I often feel I am watching a Shakespearean tragedy where most of the cast lies dead on the stage before the curtain comes down.

Aurelia Schober Plath, Sylvia's mother, must have felt angry and betrayed by both Sylvia and Ted. But surely she loved her grandchildren. Olwyn Hughes, the children's aunt, was called back from her life in France to help raise them. They were miraculously alive, after all, despite the gas, and Sylvia was dead. What would you do?

So the Hugheses walled off. They declined to let anyone reprint Plath, set Plath to music, novelize Plath, or perform Plath, except under their strict supervision. Three years ago, the Manhattan Theatre Club asked me to do a Plath poetry evening and the Hugheses refused to give permission for a reading of the poems by actors.

Maybe they were constrained by other contracts, but where openness was wanted, they closed down. And they're still careful. The Plath sanctuary remains guarded, now with the help of Frieda, who has complained about the film version of her mother's life and who wrote in a poem of her own, in the book *Wooroloo* (1998): "Wanting to breathe life into their own dead babies / . . . They scooped out her eyes to see how she saw / And bit away her tongue in tiny mouthfuls / To speak with her voice."

Frieda Hughes has had the courage to bring her mother back, not as a symbol but as a poet. Plath's poems are now published in their original versions and will have the last word. They remain remarkable. Their time has not passed. The new generations who read them may not care about their biographical underpinnings the way we did in the sixties, but they will care about their strength and craft.

We can see in this new edition what a careful constructor of poems Plath was. She weighed her commas and semicolons. She cared about what Denise Levertov and Allen Ginsberg call "breath units." She must have read her poems aloud to hear them in the air. It is touching that they were mostly written at four in the morning—"that still, blue, almost eternal hour before cockcrow, before the baby's cry, before the glassy music of the milkman, settling his bottles," as Plath put it for the BBC two months before she died, for a program that was never broadcast. "If they have anything else in common, perhaps it is that they are written for the ear, not the eye: They are poems written out loud."

I adopted this habit too, when my daughter was an infant. I love that sky blue–pink hour, do my best writing then and read what I'm writing aloud to myself, especially poetry. But the suicidal women poets who make up my heritage still trouble me.

Sylvia's suicide puts her clearly in the tradition of women who feel they must die for their transgressive acts, like Madame Bovary or Anna Karenina. In 1974, the year after I published *Fear of Flying,* the dazzlingly gifted poet Anne Sexton committed suicide too, wrapped in her mother's fur coat, inhaling carbon monoxide in the backseat of her car in Weston, Massachusetts. She had become a friend of mine and had written in my copy of *Live or Die,* "Yes, yes, let's live!"

I remember the night at the Algonquin Hotel that I sat and held her hand as she drank vodka gimlet after vodka gimlet and I struggled to keep up with her. She flirted with the waiter in case I left and she needed a companion. She would not let go of my hand. Finally at 3:30 a.m., I broke away, hoping she could sleep. I don't know whether or not she fucked the waiter.

These two daredevil poets opened the road for me. Then they closed it in another way by their self-inflicted deaths. I loved their poetry and abhorred their deaths. I wanted to smash that paradigm. Why must women artists die for their talent and self-assertion?

I never knew Sylvia Plath, but Anne was a generous mentor to me in the two years before she died. Once, when I wrote to her about my terror of publishing a second book of poems, she answered:

> *Don't dwell on the book's reception. The point is to get on with it—you have a life's work ahead of you—no point in dallying around waiting for approval. We all want it, I know, but the point is to reach out honestly—that's the whole point. I keep feeling that there isn't one poem being written by any of us—or a book or anything like that. The whole life of us writers, the whole product I guess I mean, is the one long poem—a community effort if you will. It's all the same poem. It doesn't belong to any one writer—it's God's poem perhaps. Or God's people's poem. You have the gift—and with it comes*

responsibility—you mustn't neglect or be mean to that gift—you must let it do its work. It has more rights than the ego that wants approval.

So the people who come before you transmit the energy, the chutzpah, the fearlessness. This is a community effort. "Books continue each other," as Virginia Woolf, another suicide, said in *A Room of One's Own.* You are not doing it all alone. You are standing on the shoulders of the dead. You are writing love letters to the grave. The word is a link in a human chain. You are not in this lifeboat without provisions.

Why did I hate their suicides with such vehemence? Because it seemed that every time a woman transgressed—whether in writing honestly or in embracing her sexuality—she had to punish herself. I wanted to change that. I wanted to make the world a place where women could write about their lives and live.

And what a remarkable life it is! I remember once sitting next to Carolyn Kizer on a chartered bus going to a poetry festival in Massachusetts in 1972—after my first book of poetry was out, but before *Fear of Flying* hit and changed my world. We were sitting two by two right behind the bus driver, who didn't *seem* to be listening to our conversation.

Carolyn regaled me with hilarious, possibly apocryphal, stories of famous writers she had met at literary festivals. Carolyn could be absolutely acid about the role of the woman writer as muse and literary cunt. We were allowed to be anything but colleagues.

"And then, I woke up, with Norman Mailer sitting on my face."

The bus driver suddenly swerved off the snowy road and came to a stop in a shallow ditch. Carolyn and I were both convulsed with laughter.

"But what happened after that?" I asked when I realized we were going to live.

"I have absolutely no recollection," Carolyn said. "I must have had too much to drink."

"If one woman were to tell the truth about her life the world would split open," Muriel Rukeyser had written. If proof was needed of Muriel's veracity, this was surely it.

Dear Sylvia,

Suppose I'd gone home with Ted? What would have happened? Would I have ended up committing suicide like you and Assia? I doubt it. For all my bouts of depression, I'm not inclined that way. I think growing old is more courageous. Living past your looks, your youth, and your wavy mane of hair takes real guts in a world that worships youth and disdains the witchiness of older women.

But Ted was a force of nature—a walking talking demon lover—and he knew it. You not only kissed him but bit him on the cheek, drawing blood. You were determined to leave your mark on him. Biting him was also a communication. It said: "You may be a demon lover but I am a powerful witch. My magic is stronger."

You were more of a witch than he was a warlock. To have the openness to death of your late poems, you must have had immense sexual clout. The two of you must have made the world rock on its axis when you fucked. That must have been at least half the appeal. The world split open and sucked you into its fiery core. He stayed behind but was fated never to be free of you. I could not compete with that so I fled.

Some writers are destined to have immense charisma not only in their writing but also in their lives. Byron was one. Hemingway was another. Ted was another. Anne Sexton another. You clearly had a form of female charisma that terrified men.

I think it's confusing for the writer to embody her

message as much in her personality as in her work. She never quite knows what people are responding to—the words or the icon.

We stress icons in our contemporary world because our culture has become increasingly visual. Also, we no longer have clear standards for literature. Except for a few bookworms like you and me, nobody cares about literature. I published a novel about Sappho only to discover, to my horror, that a lot of readers had no idea who Sappho was. We have jettisoned ancient history from most curricula— saying it was all about "dead white males"—so we lost Sappho as well. Would we be in Iraq if people still read Herodotus and Homer? Maybe. But at least we would see how the absurdities of history repeat themselves. Weak leaders make wars to get the people to follow them. For thousands of years, tyrants have been imprisoning dissenters, saying: It's unpatriotic to disagree with your leader in wartime. Hitler's brain, Josef Goebbels, said: Give the people an external enemy to hate and they will follow you anywhere. George W. Bush's advisers did their homework, but most people have not.

When you were alive, there was still the possi-

*bility of being an author and disdaining TV. Now,
that's another kind of suicide. We emphasize personality rather than work in our world. One has to be
photogenic, unafraid to chatter with idiots on the
screen. What on earth would Emily Dickinson have
done in the world according to Paris Hilton?*

*We scarcely trust the woman who has a pub-
lic persona and yet publishers demand it to sell
books. Charisma is rare yet we want it as a device
for PR. What contradictory qualities we demand
from writers! Women writers have a particularly
hard time because there is no way to be a public
woman without being considered a bitch, a whore or
a diva.*

You didn't live long enough to deal with all that.

What interested me when I first read the Ariel
*poems was how you broke out of the decorous good-
girl role. You confronted the world directly with
your own searing rage. It was about time a woman
raged on the page. And you gave us all the courage to
do it.*

*Ted was your demon. He opened you up. No won-
der you both hated and loved him. I found him fiercely
attractive. But in the end my loyalty was to you.*

Without adultery, is there no novel? Without sex, is there no poetry? Surely sexual energy and creative energy feed each other. Often they feel the same.

Sexual energy provokes creativity. Do poets fall in love to write about it, or does love impel creativity?

Body of a woman, white hills, white thighs, you
look like the world in your posture of surrender.

Pablo Neruda writes this in the first of his *Twenty Poems of Love and a Song of Despair*. For the poet, the lover becomes the world. The exploration of love becomes an exploration of life. Blood and love are the substance of poetry. What transmutes mere words into flesh? The power of sex. " 'Living and writing in heat'—and in fact the artist's experience lies so unbelievably close to the sexual, to its pain and its pleasure," said Rainer Maria Rilke, "that the two phenomena are really just different forms of one and the same longing and bliss."

The excitement of writing sometimes leads to sex, or at least autosex, by which I don't mean sex in a car. The excitement of words can stimulate bodily juices. And why not? The white heat that makes words assemble on the page also affects the hormones. When I feel I am telling my truth, my glands also catch fire. The muse screws.

In the days before D. H. Lawrence, James Joyce and Henry Miller, when writers were not allowed to describe sex, when the road to the bedroom had to be paved with asterisks, many of us thought that once we had the freedom to describe the sexual act, everything would be different. For a while it was.

There was a brief period of exuberant sexual freedom in American literature that began around 1967 with John Updike's *Couples,* continued with Philip Roth's *Portnoy's Complaint* and led to my own *Fear of Flying* in 1973. All these breakthroughs were really born out of Henry Miller's 1934 Paris novel, *Tropic of Cancer,* written and first published in France, that finally became a legal immigrant to America in 1962.

It was not long, however, before pornography overwhelmed literature. The same freedom that allowed real writers to chronicle the powerful sexual drives most of us experience also allowed pornographers to make fortunes off trash. And it was not long before the line between garbage and literature became hopelessly blurred.

I'm often asked what the difference is between pornography and literature? I have a simple distinction. If a piece of work is merely utilitarian, if it stimulates and facilitates only masturbation, it is pornography. If it illustrates human feelings, it is something more. That something more may not rise to the level of art but at least it aspires to it. Pornography aspires to nothing but getting the customer off. It is the massage parlor of literature. Not that there's anything wrong with getting the customer off. But its function is always strictly limited. The buyer of pornography doesn't want any hint of poetry to distract him from what Vladimir Nabokov called his "tepid lust."

Henry Miller, who was always accused by stuffy critics of being a pornographer, could not, in fact, write pornography. When he was most broke in the thirties, his lover Anaïs Nin put him in touch with a rich connoisseur of the pornographic who was willing to pay handsomely and by the page. Henry Miller didn't meet the connoisseur's standards. Too much literature apparently distracted him from his tepid lust. Nin *was* able to do it. *The Little Birds* is the result of her commission.

Most societies have been far more open to eroticism than ours. The ancient Greeks and the ancient Hindus had no problem imagining and worshipping lusty gods and goddesses. They knew that Eros was dangerous and tricky, but they also knew Eros was human. We Americans seem to need sex and contrition at the same time. Christianity and Islam have not eradicated lust but have managed to make it dirty—the worst of both worlds. No wonder we specialize in perverts and pedophilia. No wonder we have no idea what to do with teenagers but preach abstinence to them. We also have no idea what to do with ourselves. All our media use sex to sell products, yet we constantly demand that teenagers join the Anti-Sex League. Porn has become the most profitable category on the Internet while our hypocritical pundits and preachers denounce sex in the name of keeping the children pure. But how can we keep our children pure except by example? If we need sexual hypocrisy to get off, won't they?

Judaism has a less hypocritical relationship with sex than Pauline Christianity. Sex in marriage is celebrated, even mandated. But Orthodox Judaism is also full of prohibitions. And prohibitions beget hypocrisy. When a dominatrix invited me to her lair to witness sado-masochistic rites (research for one of my novels), I noticed that her waiting room was full of young men in yarmulkes. Strict prohibitions beget transgressions.

Lately, there is more sex in books by rebellious women

writers. Susie Bright and Toni Bentley, among others, are continuing the psychological exploration of sex through writing about once-forbidden subjects like anal sex, bisexuality and masochism. My brilliant former poetry student Daphne Merkin has had the courage to write about the dark delights of spanking. In prose so precise it might well be poetry, she has dared to report desires we still experience despite their political incorrectness.

D. H. Lawrence notwithstanding, I've always thought that the most revealing sex takes place inside the head. How else could the demon lover conquer when usually he turns out to be an ordinary guy? Fantasy has always fueled my hottest encounters. Without fantasy, sex is not much more than friction.

In *Fear of Flying*, I wanted to slice open my protagonist's head and reveal the fantasies within. There was far more fantasy than reality. Most of the sexual escapades were disappointing compared to the lavishness of Isadora's fantasy life. Perhaps that's the case with most people. Our fantasies are a shortcut to revealing ourselves. Remember Virginia Woolf's reaction to James Joyce's *Ulysses:* ". . . a queasy undergraduate scratching his pimples." She found the book disgusting. It aroused her class prejudices: ". . . an illiterate, underbred book . . . the book of a self-taught working man."

The physicality of *Ulysses,* which has delighted so many readers, made her squirm.

What were Virginia Woolf's fantasies? I think we see them in *Orlando,* where she imagines herself effortlessly switching genders with the centuries. She is always the aesthete, the bodiless romantic, whichever gender she inhabits. It is never easy to see her as a totally physical being. She is Ariel to James Joyce's Caliban.

The hardest thing for me about writing sex scenes is that I know when writing them that I am revealing myself totally. There's no place to hide. My fantasies reveal me no matter how I ornament them with eighteenth-century wigs or sixteenth-century chopines or ancient Greek tunics. My fantasies *are* me.

In my twenties, I used to ride the train from Heidelberg to Frankfurt four days a week to visit my analyst. In the rocking of the train, in my early morning drowsiness, I allowed my fantasies to bubble up into consciousness. Suppose on that train I saw a man who moved me, whose face, whose walk, whose smell stimulated lust? Suppose the train entered a gallery or grew suddenly dark and it was possible for us to make love secretly, without ever knowing each other's names? That's how the fantasy of the Zipless Fuck was born.

For the longest time, women in novels had to be

severely punished for their sexual expression. Anna Karenina and Madame Bovary died for their sins. That archetype extended far into the twentieth century with a slight change: Loss of a child substituting for death itself. I am thinking of *The Good Mother,* by Sue Miller, and *August Is a Wicked Month*, by Edna O'Brien. We are still not entirely comfortable with sexuality in women going unpunished.

The most promiscuous woman character in *Sex and the City* is rebuked with breast cancer. For all that Samantha bears it heroically, breast cancer is clearly a variant of the old dies-for-her-sins paradigm. I've already talked about my own strong unconscious pull toward that paradigm and my deliberate desire not to fulfill it. This is why writing a novel is such a profound self-exploration. In the process, you discover how deeply societal myths have marked you. If you wish to change the world, you must first change yourself. Nowhere is this clearer than in writing about sex.

When D. H. Lawrence wrote in the twenties about Lady Chatterley and Mellors twining gentians in each other's pubic hair, it was as shocking as it would be silly now. When Lawrence used the word "cunt" it was unheard of. Now it is commonplace.

One of the qualities I liked best about Susan Minot's

lovely novel *Rapture*, which tells the story of two former lovers briefly reuniting sexually, was her ability to get inside intimacy without using four-letter words. This may sound like odd praise coming from a writer who tried to domesticate four-letter words in her early books. But sexual language is more common now, so freshness must be sought by other means. Any writer who writes about sex will inevitably come up against the dilemma that a culture that denigrates sex will have mostly pejorative words for the genitals and for acts of love. "Fucking" is a violent term that means both intercourse and submission. "Cunt" is both a term of abuse and a label for the female genital. "Prick" is also a term of abuse. Our language of sex tells us how much we hate and fear sex even as we yearn for it. It takes a great deal of sensitivity and skill to make sexual language new. English has dirty words like "fuck" and "cunt" and medical words like "intercourse" and "vagina." Often writers are tempted to make up new words, like James Joyce referring to Molly Bloom's "plump mellow yellow smellow melons . . . in their mellow yellow furrow, with obscure prolonged provocative melonsmellonous osculation."

The language with which my characters talk about sex reveals them as much as anything. A woman who says "down there" is a different creature from a woman who says "my cunt." When I did a brief stint in Eve Ensler's *Vagina Monologues* in New York, I was given the monologue of an uptight old lady who could not say the word "vagina." She could hardly say "down there." Impersonating that character, I really began to understand how hard it was for certain people to deal with spoken sex. Our sexual speech reflects our discomfort with the whole subject.

Part of the great fun I had in writing *Fanny* was to play with all the rambunctious sexual words that were current in the eighteenth century. Once you have your pick of *pillicock, picklock* and *privy member,* how can you ever be satisfied with a mere *prick* again? Once you have *cunnikin, divine monosyllable, altar of hymen, belle chose, centre-of-bliss, cream-jug, Cupid's cloister, quim, quimsby* or *quivive,* why on earth would you want *snatch?*

When I have trouble writing about sex with freshness, I retrieve abandoned words from the past—words like "quim" or "quente"—or I content myself with describing the yearning for sex without the mechanics. The yearning is probably the most important part anyway. I find the most difficult aspect of writing about sex to be evoking the spiritual connection between people. Sometimes the things that are most important in life are beyond words.

Not long ago I went to the opening of a movie in which I appeared as a cultural commentator. It was a documentary called *Inside Deep Throat* and basically it took the position that this 1972 porno film had permanently changed the world.

That's not at *all* how I remember it. I remember the late sixties and early seventies as a time of exuberance and hope. Pornography was only a tiny part of it. Many of us believed that once people were no longer hypocritical about sex, they would no longer be hypocritical about other things—like politics. How naive that was! We never imagined a world where right-wing ideologues might jerk off on their computers and then go to Congress and vote against sex education for teenagers. We foolishly believed that *all* hypocrisy would vanish once people stopped being hypocritical about sex. It's not that simple. Hypocrisy is always with us. We now live in a world where sex is everywhere but has been utterly degraded. That was the last thing I expected The Sixties to promote.

All the more reason to write about sex honestly today. Sex motivates. Why pretend otherwise? Close-ups on the genitals are sometimes needed, sometimes not. Sometimes close-ups only blur the view.

And what about the fear of disease? How has that

changed sex in our time? Larry Kramer has written movingly about the recklessness of young gay men growing up in the age of the AIDS "cocktail," confident that pills exist for every malady. Young people never believe in the possibility of their own deaths. That's one reason old men can send them to war.

Sex has the unparalleled power to make us absurd to ourselves. It also has the power to make us understand transcendence.

When it is ecstatic, nothing is more powerful than sex. And nothing is more difficult to capture in words than transcendence. It's not only because sex is embarrassing to many people, but also because ecstasy implies loss of control. This is difficult to acknowledge.

Nobody seems to talk about ecstasy these days. Sex is always talked about in terms of control. Teenage girls giving blow jobs for power not pleasure, middle-aged women boasting of their boy toys, men modelizing for the sake of show. Only gay men admit to being in pursuit of ecstasy, but often their ecstasy is fueled by drugs. If you go back and look at D. H. Lawrence, who has been discovered and abandoned so many times that he bores most literary folk, you'll see that his great revolution was to get ecstasy down on the page, and ecstasy cannot exist without loss of control.

She could do nothing. She could no longer harden and grip for her own satisfaction upon him. She could only wait, wait and moan in spirit as she felt him withdrawing, withdrawing and contracting, coming to the terrible moment when he would slip out of her and be gone. Whilst all her womb was open and soft, and softly clamouring like a sea-anemone under the tide, clamouring for him to come in again and make a fulfillment for her. She clung to him in unconscious passion and he never quite slipped from her, and she felt the soft bud of him within her stirring, and strange rhythms flushing up into her with a strange rhythmic growing motion, swelling and swelling until it filled all her cleaving consciousness, and then began the unspeakable motion that was not really motion, but pure deepening whirlpools of sensation swirling deeper and deeper through all her tissue and consciousness, till she was one perfect concentric fluid of feeling, and she lay there crying in inarticulate cries.

It's so easy to make fun of Lawrence (which I have done myself) and so hard to be open to his grasp of ecstasy. His gerunds were not old hat then (Joyce got all gerundy too, in Molly Bloom's voice) and his sea anemones were not yet clichés. His deliberate repetitions had not yet been parodied. If you can overlook all that in *Chatterley* and appreciate his depiction of sexless, lifeless marriage, you will see that he is one of the great novelists of marriage. He understood the longing for ecstasy. He was not afraid to give sex its due. We have fallen a long way since then. Sex is everywhere in media, but ecstasy is absent. Many literary novelists shy away from sex because it's become a pornographic cliché. But it doesn't need to be. In Philip Roth's repellently brilliant novel *Sabbath's Theatre,* Mickey Sabbath's rape of the cleaning lady at his friend's New York co-op becomes a powerful signal of his decline into chaos. First he rampages through his friend's wife's lingerie drawers. Then he desecrates his friend's daughter's belongings. Finally, in case we have any doubt about what kind of guest Sabbath is, he sodomizes the cleaning lady. Sometimes only a character's sexuality will give us the interior view.

· · ·

I tried to write about the role of sex in my life in *Fear of Fifty*, but I realize now, in my sixties, that I didn't know the half of it. Until you get wise enough (or old enough) to understand sex as a whole-body experience, you know nothing. All my life I had heard about tantric sex and I thought it was utter bullshit—raising the kundalini, yoga poses in tandem, mysteries of the East and all that rot. Most of our sexuality is so focused on the stiff prick that we have no idea what to do when that becomes occasionally problematic as it does with age. You can become a Viagra junkie or you can create other ways of making love. The deliciousness of skin, of oral sex, of sex without homage to the divine Lawrentian "phallos" can be a revelation. Is this what it means to become androgynous—that buzzword of the seventies? Is this what it means to be bisexual? There's a great deal to be said for both androgyny and bisexuality, then. Whatever breaks our fixation on the genitals and turns us into entire bodies linked to entire minds enhances sex. The best Italian lover I ever had could practically make me come by stroking my neck.

The married poet who shook with fear, then fucked me with a stiff cock, was no sort of lover at all. A lover makes love with words, with stroking, with laughter.

Anxiety ruins sex. Which may be why married people can have great sex—as can longtime lovers, or longtime friends. Music, stroking, scent, poetry—these things are far more important than a stiff prick.

I only realized when my husband had to take heart medication and could not tolerate Viagra that we were able to discover things we never knew before. He could have a whole-body orgasm while giving oral sex—his orgasm triggered by mine. He could feel electric shocks down his spine—as if the kundalini were rising. And I could feel them in my spine too—so connected are we. When we were able to have genital sex after that, he said, "It feels so localized compared to before." Intercourse produces an orgasm in the pelvic area, but other kinds of sex produce it all over the body—and mind. Or maybe it is just our desire to merge that is so strong. In bed we laugh and argue and have fun. We talk about everything. He provokes me with his jokes. I provoke him with mine. By the time we go skin to skin, we are so close already that we have no boundaries.

We need to take days out of our "normal" lives. We need to go to Venice or India or Machu Picchu. We need to dock our sailboat in an unknown port. We need to touch each other riding on waves.

. . .

Before Martha Stewart was a convicted felon or had sprouted synthetic angel wings from going to jail for a few months, she was a college classmate of mine who became a caterer who became a conglomerate and who was famous in Connecticut for treating her employees like disposable paper plates. I have no idea whether she still goes around telling everyone I ruined her marriage, but I do wish I had the sexual power she attributes to me. Actually, I believe I had very little to do with the problems in her marriage. I was just a pawn in a power struggle, a spear-carrier in her opera.

Simone de Beauvoir, one of my literary heroines, once wrote that when she embarked on writing about her life, she felt she had begun "a somewhat rash adventure." It cannot be otherwise. One's life is full of mortifications, blind fumblings in the dark. It is terrible to have to write them down—especially when you have pledged honesty— to the point of embarrassment.

Martha Kostyra was very pretty when I first saw her at Barnard. I knew she "had made" *Glamour* magazine's college issue, an envied desideratum of my day. She was blond and tall and had married while still in school. Like most Barnard girls, she was fiercely independent and had a life apart from the college. Barnard was no bubble. In those days it was a commuter college. Lots of students were married and some had kids. It was a college for smart outsiders—which is probably why it has produced so many writers.

I didn't meet her again until she had become a caterer in Connecticut. I was living in the next town, and we had several friends in common whose sons' bar mitzvahs she catered, with elegant hors d'oeuvres like caviar wasted on thirteen-year-olds. She had a rare attention to detail. Her food was delicious. It was also extremely expensive.

Her husband was a publisher of illustrated books, who was just then enjoying a great success with a book called *Gnomes*. It had humorous illustrations of all sorts of little creatures—gnomes, elves, sprites and fairies. Each of these creatures satirized a recognizable contemporary creature complete with his or her accoutrements.

Gnomes was the sort of book no one could have predicted would be a blockbuster. Both the author and the illustrator were obscure, but somehow the satire and fantasy worked. And now there were gnome dolls, gnome cereals, gnome clothes, gnome pop-up books.

One night Martha, her husband, Andy Stewart, and my third husband, Jonathan Fast, and I were at the same dinner party in the country. Her husband began talking about doing a sequel to *Gnomes*—a book about witches. I had just published *Fanny: Being the True History of the Adventures of Fanny Hackabout-Jones,* in which Fanny becomes a witch, a pirate, a highwaywoman and a high-class eighteenth-century London hooker. I had steeped myself in research about witchcraft and paganism for *Fanny.* I was convinced that most of the things written about witches and witch hunts were dead wrong. In my research notebook for *Fanny,* I'd written:

> *Witchcraft—another name for the survival of paganism under the cover of Christianity in Medieval and Renaissance Europe. Paganism—never really extinguished, Figures of the horned God or the Mother Goddess never really replaced. They lingered on but had to go underground to survive. Witches' covens were pagan rituals practiced in the fields, under the full moon. Women were skyclad—or nude—and the peeping Christians saw iniquity where there was nature worship. It was a case of projection of lascivious desires onto innocent ancient practices.*

The publisher was intrigued. Here I was, an author ready to write—and passionate. The research was done.

Publishers love that. They always suspect we will be dilatory in writing books and usually they are right. We are so scared of being judged that we look for every excuse to procrastinate. Here was a quick book by a famous writer.

Of course we both overlooked the fact that gnomes were fantasy creatures and witches were real. Nobody had been burned for being a gnome. Women had been burned all over Europe and America for being witches.

From then on, the Stewarts wooed me and Jon, sent us beautiful books, baby gifts (Molly was two) and invitations to dinner. Their dinners were spectacular theatricals—vodka bottles encased in flower-filled blocks of ice, hand-dipped candles, roses from their own bushes, eggs from their own hens. There were plenty of rich people in Connecticut then as now, but nobody lived like that—but the Stewarts.

Andy Stewart often spoke of his "chores"—collecting the eggs, cleaning the henhouse, weeding the vegetable patch. He seemed somewhat bitter. And he was extremely flirtatious with me.

Then it happened that he and I were both due to be at the Frankfurt Book Fair at the same time, and when I arrived I found a note from him saying, "I can't wait to see you." I thought nothing of it. I had a hellish schedule ahead. Both my German and Italian publishers had paid for my trip, and my French and Dutch publishers also had claims on my time. I spent the five long days in the lobby of the Frankfurter Hof giving interviews, literally not leaving the hotel till after sundown. My mailbox was stuffed with requests from journalists, but there were also messages from Andy urging "Call me!" and giving his room number.

"Hotel rooms inhabit a separate moral universe," says Tom Stoppard in *Night and Day*. The same should be said of the Frankfurt Book Fair. Nothing said or done there should morally count. Everyone is exhausted, sure they are missing the best parties and anxious about their futures. Hell will be the Frankfurt Book Fair. You'll know it's hell because you'll never be able to leave. And desperate authors and exhausted publishers will surround you.

What happened next is not hard to imagine. I got many romantic missives from the Andy of my classmate and found myself in his room one night. (We were staying in the same hotel, the Frankfurter Hof.) In his room, I got to hear endlessly about Martha.

"She doesn't only want to control everything everyone *eats* but what everyone *thinks* at every moment," he said. "When I'm home, I have endless farm duties and household duties. I have no life of my own. Everything is about *her*."

And in my view, everything was indeed about her. His romancing me was about her, his conversation about her, his rage about her. Rage is not a good basis for sex. Nor is revenge. He was getting his revenge for his chores. He was getting even with her about things I couldn't even imagine.

I remember him as big and blond and enthusiastic. I know he pulled the comforters to the floor and it was there that we tangled. Whatever people may say of the delights of adultery, there are always these extra people in the room observing. You are playing to them more than to your partner. And all the while your demon is mocking you.

"You couldn't be happy with me—you had to drag this big blond one to bed? You'll live to regret it. The wife's a problematic enemy—or soon will be. What a pathetically easy lay you are—a few handwritten notes and you fall into bed? Or onto the floor? What's the matter with you?"

"But isn't he cute?"

"Cute and a token will get you on the subway. Besides he's not cute enough for all the trouble this will cause!

You and Jonathan may have an 'open marriage'—if such a thing exists—but the Stewarts are thoroughly bourgeois. He cheats and she pretends not to know. They live in Westport, after all. Wait and see! You just wanted to show her who's boss. But she'll *get* you."

This demon sounds suspiciously like my father, but he is always, alas, right.

Right before I left for summer school in Florence, when I was nineteen, my father said, "I have one piece of advice for you: Never drink grappa with an Italian man."

Of course that was the very first thing I proceeded to do after Italian literature class at the Torre di Bello-sguardo. In fact, I defiantly drank grappa with every Italian man I met. I drank grappa on trains, on motorcycles, in little bars along the Arno. Later on, when I was older, I drank grappa on vintage sailboats and in grand hotels. I am not sorry for my defiance—only grateful I survived it without catching any communicable diseases. And what was I looking for in that glass of grappa? An old-fashioned cordial: love. I never found it there.

· · ·

In the morning I crept out of Stewart's room hoping not to be seen by anyone. But the deed had been done. My one-night stand must have gone home and immediately told the wife he'd slept with me—which was apparently the whole point of the exercise.

From then on she never lost an opportunity to tell the world: ERICA JONG RUINED MY MARRIAGE. ERICA JONG RUINED MY LIFE. She told mutual friends, trashy journalists, Barnard alumnae who had gathered to celebrate her. Sometimes she said, "That woman ruined my life!" Whenever she saw me, she gave me a killing look.

And who could blame her? I was wrong. My demon made me do it. Sleeping with married men is always trouble. I have forsworn it.

If I could take this incident back, I would. My regret is Dantean—and not just because Martha keeps telling tabloid journalists about this twenty-six-year-old gaffe and denouncing me as if she had no faults herself. But I accept the blame. I was always besotted by books and anyone who made them. Remember the story of Paolo and Francesca in Dante's *Inferno*?

Galeotto fu il libro e chi lo scrisse
That book was our panderer
and him that made it . . .

Beware of books. They are more than innocent as-
semblages of paper and ink and string and glue. If they
are any good, they have the spirit of the author within.
Authors are rogues and ruffians and easy lays. They are
gluttons for sweets and savories. They devour life and
always want more. They have sap, spirit, sex. Books *are*
panderers. The Jews are not wrong to worship books. A
real book has pheromones and sprouts grass through its
cover. Whitman knew that.

I pick up my facsimile edition of *Leaves of Grass,*
given to me by the previous publisher. This is the same
edition Whitman sent to Emerson.

I read:

*The English language befriends the grand American
expression. . . . It is brawny enough and limber enough
and full enough . . . it is the powerful language of
resistance . . . it is the dialect of common sense. It is
the speech of the proud and melancholy races and of
all who aspire. It is the chosen tongue to express
growth faith self-esteem freedom justice equality
friendliness amplitude prudence decision and courage.
It is the medium that shall well nigh express the inex-
pressible. . . . The proof of a poet is that his country
absorbs him as affectionately as he has absorbed it.*

The writer's job is to absorb. Plenitude and amplitude are our watchwords. We are "hankering, gross,
mystical, nude." We know that mistakes are part of wisdom and wisdom is made of plenty of foolishness.

If you learn to loaf and invite your soul, you will
make mistakes you wish you could cancel with a word.
You cannot. You can only confess and hope for the
mercy of heaven.

"Oh, come on," my editor says. "You don't regret any
of those things, Without them, you wouldn't be the person you are today. You might not want to do them now,
but those adventures were part of your life. Don't dis-
own them. You are a seductress. You always wanted to be
a seductress."

"O.K.," I say. I realize he's right—which is why
he's the editor for me. The most uncomfortable things
I did, I did knowing in my gut that I would write
about them.

"Amen!" says my demon. "Amen!"

And thunder breaks and lightning flashes because
demons aren't allowed to say "Amen."

Whenever I see Martha on TV, in tabloids, in maga-
zines, I think, Does she trust anyone? It's hard to trust,

and I didn't make it any easier for her. When you can't trust anyone, there's no choice but to wind up alone. A blasted marriage can also blast your heart.

When I met Ken, my fourth husband, I was not good at trusting men. I had been hurt too many times—even though I now see that a lot of the pain was self-inflicted. I had made what I thought was a lifelong commitment to Molly's father, Jonathan, and when we both blew that (open marriage is a crock) I developed a headache that lasted for six months. I couldn't imagine ever trusting anyone—or myself—again.

Ken struck me as the smartest man I'd ever met and the most anxious. When he tipped his chair back in the restaurant we first dined in together, I thought, He's going to smash his head open and then where will I be?

"Don't do that!"

"Do what?" he asked in a total fog. He rattled on describing his life to me—how he got kicked out of Brown for not going to class because he was doing drugs, how he made movies for a while with Brian De Palma, how he went back to school and law school and fell in love with his métier, how he married twice, then lived with someone for ten years and helped raise her daughter, how he initially didn't want to meet me because I was "famous" but was glad he did. All his feelings tumbled out. He was not playing games. He was all there.

When you have been dating the sort of withholding men who go for well-known women, this is refreshing. Besides, he was really cute—big and bearish and bearded with warm brown eyes and shaggy brown hair. But what I really liked was his openness. On our second date, he took me to a Yiddish play and watched me intently to see how much *mamaloschen* I got.

"This is a test, isn't it?"

He nodded yes.

"Well, did I pass?"

He nodded yes again.

If you had asked me whether I knew Yiddish, I would not have said yes, but apparently I knew more than I thought.

When I told him I could never marry again because it would interfere with my writing, he swore it would not. When I hesitated, he offered me a written release. He scribbled on a napkin: "Write anything you want about me!"

He knew who I was and loved me. But still I found it hard to trust. For ten years we kept our property separate—except for the apartment we bought together. But little by little, separate stashes seemed a waste of time. Inevitably, things got mixed and muddled. Then, on our tenth anniversary, we burned our prenup in a wok with all our dearest friends watching.

Shortly after that, Ken nearly died of an aortic aneurism. I rushed him to New York Hospital where he was lucky enough to find on duty a surgeon who specialized in aortic repair. It wasn't his time. He survived. The least important thing was whether our assets were mixed. By the time he recovered, our relationship had gone to another level. I knew I didn't want to wake up or go to sleep without him. Money was the least of it.

Even Barbra Streisand remarried not long after she asked me at a party, "How come you always remarry?"

"You gotta trust somebody," I said.

"But where do you meet men?"

"I don't know. I just like men."

"Is that all there is to it?" she asked.

"Who knows?"

But trusting yourself to trust somebody is key.

For me, poetry always comes fast and furiously when I'm in love—or at least lust. It's notoriously hard for poets to tell the difference. When I first fell in love with my husband Ken, I wrote poems for him.

A Venetian cad even inspired me to attempt love poems in Italian. Since he used to call me *pane caldo* (hot bread), I already had the central metaphor.

The point is—lust provokes poetry. It can be lust for a man, a woman, a child or God, but it's hard to propel the recalcitrant pen along the recalcitrant page without it. Think of Shakespeare's sonnets, or Petrarch's, or Edna St. Vincent Millay's.

Why is lust so critical? I really don't know. Our bodies may not last forever, but while we have them, they are heat-seeking missiles. We are hot-blooded mammals and whatever makes us hotter inspires us to poetry, song, fiction, fecundity. I don't suppose reptiles write love poetry. But maybe they do and we just can't understand it. When the sun shines on the crocodile's skin, perhaps she sings strange songs of love with her toothy mouth. She loves the sun the way I love men. I tried women a couple of times, but it just seemed too cozy. It was like hot cocoa and angel food cake. Men are more like pungent hunks of meat. Their bulk, their smell, their muscles turn me on. Women are too delicate, too sweet, too (dare I say it?) empathic. There—I have said it. My lust is politically incorrect. Whenever I had sex with a woman, I

liked it fine—but without the fierce drive to do it again.
As you age, heterosexual men grow scarce (your contemporaries die off), but there are so many lovable women.
Who knows what the future holds? I have learned never
to say never.

Once I was in lust with a poet I cannot name. He was
and is married. I was not at the time. He wrote me the
sexiest letters full of black garter belts and rosy rumps
and black stockings and dirty poems and references to
The Story of O—which we both found sexy—even
though I am not a masochist (though he may well be a
sadist). Of course I hardly knew him, but I knew his
work. It was also highly erotic, enormously yearning—
both the poems and novels. I made plans to meet him in
London while I was promoting a book for my British
publisher, who put me up at a circular-bedroomed suite
at the Ritz on Piccadilly.

Waiting for this assignation, I ruminated about the
poet. I had made the date with him six months before
during a lull in my erotic life. I had just spent most of the
summer in Venice, where I fell in love with an adorable
Italian who sailed his vintage sailboat down the Dalmatian coast but would never take me along. (Did he have a
Croatian cookie on the side?)

So I met the sexy British poet in the sexy hotel suite in

London. His letters had been erotic masterpieces, but in life he had an ugly little cardboard suitcase and he was so nervous he shook. His teeth were Englishly crooked, his shoulders were hunched and he smelled of moth-balled tweed and cheap pipe tobacco. His eyes were intensely black and his hair was white. Whenever I looked at him, all I could think of was that he was not the sailing Italian.

The hotel intimidated the poet with its elegance, so, at his suggestion, we went out to dinner in a cruddy restaurant in the neighborhood where he ordered sour plonk. (Not that they had any other kind at that dive.) He couldn't eat, but he drank a lot. The food was awful, so I suggested we go back to my suite where we ordered champagne and hors d'oeuvres.

He suggested we read each other poems since that was how we met—through poetry. But he couldn't stop trembling even after all that booze.

He read. I read. We talked a little. He spoke of his son, who had been accused of rape "by a rich Jewish girl, with a posh Hampstead house and family connections."

"You know, of course, that I am Jewish. You seem not to like my tribe much."

"Oh, no," he protested. "It was just this girl who tried to put my son in jail."

"You're sure he didn't rape her?"

"Of course. He wouldn't do a thing like that."

I decided he was an anti-Semite and I that wouldn't sleep with him. I protested that I felt ill and would he leave?

"There's no train till tomorrow. I'll sleep on the couch."

"Why don't you find another hotel?"

"I can't afford it. My wife will know if I put it on a credit card. She's a schoolteacher and she pays the bills."

"Where did you *say* you went?"

"Not here," he said pathetically. "I said I had to meet my publisher in London. I said I was staying in his guest room. Please let me stay here. We're poets, after all. We're not bourgeois."

Speak for yourself, I wanted to say. As for me, I got them "Bourgeois Blues"—with apologies to Leadbelly.

I went into my circular bedroom and locked the heavy concave paneled door. I removed my make-up and washed my face. Why the hell wouldn't he leave? I put on a bathrobe and thought about him. Was I being too cruel? Was he perhaps just depressed about his son possibly going to jail? Was I seeing anti-Semitism where it was not? Was I being oversensitive? I can be very oversensitive when it comes to anti-Semitism. And England—as my English cousins can tell you—is rife with it. As for the poet, I no longer even *liked* him, let alone lusted for him. But here he was.

I read for a while, then grew upset about his presence in the other room. I wanted him to leave. He made me anxious. I imagined him on the couch, wrapped in his cheap imitation Aquascutum raincoat. I felt like La Belle Dame sans Merci.

I peeked out the door. He looked wretched on the couch, still shivering. Men are so quick to take trains or planes hoping to cheat on their wives, but they really can't cope. When we decide to cheat, we *do* it. They just get pathetic or impotent or trembly.

"How *are* you?" I asked, knowing the answer.

"Lonely. Can I sleep with you? I promise nothing will happen."

Nothing will happen, they say, stepping out of their pants. Nothing will happen, they promise, sticking in their cocks. Nothing will happen, they say, "I'll take it out before I come."

So I relented. He got into my bed. Within seconds he had stopped shaking, had an erection and was covering it with a brand-new condom.

"Just this once."

I thought: That's what they all say. I thought: I really should throw him out. But since he had a clean foil-wrapped condom, I let him fuck me once—out of pity—just to get it over with. I felt numb. Pity is not erotic.

He was an anti-Semite—I was sure of it. I hated myself for this, but maybe now he'd leave. No such luck.

Thank God, Morpheus arrived and I fell asleep. My greatest blessing is to be able to sleep anywhere no matter what. I don't know whether he did. I awoke to find him making furious notes in his notebook, lying on the couch in the living room.

Great, I thought, I'll be in his next book. The only good part is nobody reads poetry!

But before my first interview, I spent about an hour in the bath, scrubbing him off. At that point, I never wanted to see him again. But I have his raunchy letters for my archive.

Oh yes. And copies of my own to him.

Some people are better in books than in life. Reading his poems, I could imagine him a dark demon to be seduced. Meeting him in life, he just became another tin pot Casanova.

.   .   .

I can't finish this catalogue of lovers demonic and un- unless I write about Dart (not his real name), who started in the Social Register and wound up selling meat from a truck.

He was from Darien and Fifth Avenue and he had four names with a roman numeral after them. He entered my life by deliberately skidding off my driveway in a snowstorm and left it five years later when I got tired of his drugs and deceptions and the weapons he kept under my bed.

My driveway in Connecticut is steep and I thought he had skidded accidentally. Only later did he admit that he had buried his car in a snowbank to bury himself in me. And I didn't know about his love affair with guns.

"Jewish girls and guns don't go together," said my friend Grace. When I think of the disasters that might have happened, I shudder.

When he was in his twenties, Dart was gorgeous. He had sandy hair, ice-blue eyes, huge biceps, shapely legs and a cock that went on forever—though it listed to the left, in the opposite direction from his parents' politics. Part of attraction is novelty—and Dart was a novelty in my life. He had broken his parents' hearts by not going to Yale—though all his ancestors had. He embraced the actor's craft but performed mostly offstage. He could convince any girl into bed—after which he got bored. Conquest versus closeness.

Will the sexes ever agree? I doubt it—not as long as the hormones flow.

Fast forward a decade and a half: My daughter Molly and husband Ken were out somewhere and I was taking an afternoon nap in my Connecticut house, where our bedroom is on the first floor. Drowsing in and out of sleep—naps are rare for me—I hear a ring at the door. I stumble out of bed without my glasses and open up. Before me is a blurry tall figure.

"I can't believe it, baby—you don't remember me!"

"Let me get my glasses."

I put them on and there is Dart, whom I haven't seen for years. He much the worse for wear—with a paunch, a slight sway to his back and a seductive voice that announces he has no idea his hunkiness has fled. When I knew him he was tall and buff and blond—a goy god to make Jewish girls weak in the knees.

"What's up, baby? Can I come in?"

"Sure." I walk over to the round dining-room table and he sits down next to me.

"How's the actor's vagabond life?"

"Not much acting but a lot of vagabonding," he says.

"Catch me up."

"I can't believe I lost the only true love of my life," he moans.

"And who was that?"

"You, baby. I just didn't appreciate it at the time. I'd give anything to have you back."

"I'm married to Ken. It's a good marriage. I'm not in the market for reunions."

"Lucky for you, baby. I have two little boys and my wife just threw me out."

"I never knew about the marriage or the kids. You didn't send engraved announcements."

"Should have written you," Dart says, putting his face on the dining-room table, "but I was so ashamed."

"Tell me about your boys."

And then he proceeded to tell a long story about himself and Calliope (a mile-high Greek girl with "humongous tits," according to Dart), the birth of the boys, how wonderful he was to her when Calliope was pregnant, his trouble getting work, his fantasies that Calliope was fucking the owner of the diner where she worked and doing a cornucopia of drugs, his futile attempts to get sober, his futile efforts to save the marriage, and other bullshit.

Being Dart, he was probably fucking three other girls and coming home to her all weepy to spend her money.

Once, I had been willing to believe whatever Dart said, but now it all sounded fake to me. Just as he had once gotten me to take care of him, he now wanted me to rescue his boys. I was not in the foster-mom business, though I was afraid if I met them, they'd melt my resolve.

"You have to meet them. Telemachus is brilliant—we call him Telly—and Ari is so adorable, you'd die. I know now what you felt for Molly. I empathize so. Too bad I had no understanding of parenthood at the time."

"So what do you *want*, Dart?"

"Nothin', baby, just to see you again and tell you you're the love of my life. I really goofed. I really fucked up."

"Where did this revelation come from?"

"I've just been thinking about us. I could do so much better now. I'm a father now. I understand so much more."

What was he thinking? Did he really think he could waltz back in here and rekindle the flame with a few confessions of fault? Was he insane? I was a different person. I knew his jive. I was married, seriously married to a serious person I loved, a person I could count on, a person who could count on me. And Dart had lost his looks, his youth. He was no longer twenty-six, as he'd been when we met. He might still have that indefatigable cock, but that wasn't enough anymore. Couldn't he see it?

Obviously not.

"Baby, I miss you."

"Well, you'll just have to keep missing me, I'm afraid." I got up from the table and walked to the door. "It was nice seeing you again."

Dart took a proprietary tone. "Is he treatin' you right? Is he takin' care of you like I did?"

"Dart—stop kidding yourself with this act. You never took care of me."

"But I did, baby, I did the best I could." Now he was standing next to the door with me.

He put out his large hand and stroked my cheek. Nothing stirred at his touch. And I had written a whole book about him! Four hundred pages—more . . .

"Nothing so dead as a dead love," my friend Grace used to say.

"Don't you remember the fun we had—in Venice, in Split, in Dubrovnik? Remember that drive along the Dalmatian coast in the Zastava that we held together with wire hangers?

"Remember that trip to Japan where you did those lectures? Remember Kyoto? Remember the thousand and one Buddhas?"

I nodded.

"And remember that time in Venice when we hung out in Palazzo Barbaro with Ed White and his friends and John Malcolm Brinnin?"

"Lots of those friends are dead of AIDS."

"Oh, baby, I didn't know."

"Have you been under a rock?"

I remembered my suspicion that Dart was cheating on me with some of my gay friends. For Dart, sex was a commodity. He would do whatever he needed to do to be part of a group. He was that insecure. Of course, I have no evidence other than my paranoia.

"Take care of yourself," I said, knowing he was incapable of it.

"Can I call you from time to time?"

"Why not?"

"Baby, I want you to see my truck."

I looked out the door and saw this small white truck with a cab and a closed caboose.

"What happened to the car I bought you?"

"I gave it to Calliope. She needed a car to get to work.

I also gave her all the furniture and books—including some of yours. I'm sorry, baby."

If he said "baby" one more time I'd scream.

But for some reason I walked outside with him to the truck. He opened the locker in back and cold mist poured out.

"You see this meat?" he asked.

In the truck were enormous quantities of vacuum-packed frozen foods—shrimp, crab cakes, steaks, pork chops, racks of lamb, bacon, yams, clams, pizzas, paella.

"All the meat is restaurant-quality prime and all the fish is flash-frozen at sea. I'd love to share it with you," he said as if he were giving me a present.

He began rummaging in the locker and took out masses of food, samples of each. He stacked it all in a carton and began to walk toward the front door.

"I want you to have this, baby."

He walked back in the house, rearranged my freezer, packed it in and then he began to cry.

"I wish I could give it to you, baby, I really wish I could, but I'm stony broke."

"How much, Dart?"

"Well, it's six hundred dollars' worth of food, but four hundred will do."

I wrote him a check as he wept.

"Baby, I can't thank you enough," he said. "You'll love the clams. I know you will."

When Molly and Ken came home, I was frying crab cakes—a most unaccustomed activity. Usually, Ken is the weekend chef and I am decidedly *sous-chef* and cleaner-upper.

They both looked suspicious but I was embarrassed to tell them what had happened. So I pretended I'd bought the food in New York and brought it up to the country.

After a week of steaks, paella, clams, pork chops and racks of lamb, my daughter looked at me with her most mocking expression and said, "Père de Step and I think that meat has a dirty little secret. Whad'you do? Knock off a caterer? You'd better tell us where you got it."

"I'm trying to learn to cook."

"You must be kidding," Moll said. "It's a little late to play happy housewife. I remember how panicked I used to get on the nanny's night off that I'd starve to death!"

It was true. No sooner did Margaret disappear up the driveway than Molly used to ask, wistfully, "Momma, can you cook?"

"Of course!" I'd say defensively before calling the pizza place or the Chinese takeout.

So I finally told Molly and Ken about Dart and his frozen meat. I lowered the price of the order, though— as I do when telling Ken about designer clothes from Bergdorf's. And Molly, of course, took the story for her next book. Ken also dines out on both versions whenever he gets a chance.

"Meat from a Truck" is what I would call this chapter if Dart were still worth writing a novel about. But the symbolism is just too obvious. The meat is no longer fresh.

Ever since Freud opined that the artist longs for fame, glory and the love of beautiful women, people have assumed that fame means the same thing for women as it does for men. Famous men may find tootsies, gold diggers and plaster casters at every turn, but famous women attract louts, losers and men of indeterminate sexuality who want to publicly prove themselves. Maybe it's different for actresses—acting is one field that heightens femininity—but the well-known woman writer is likely to wind up like the romance writer in Fay Weldon's *Life and Loves of a She-Devil:* Seduced and abandoned and broke.

I consider it a miracle that I met Ken, who understood me and loved me anyway and wasn't intimidated by my ridiculous public image. He deflates my diva act with laughter whenever I pull it on him.

"*Ich kenst du,*" (I know you) he'll say in Yiddish when I get on my high horse and lecture him about politics, global warming or the vicissitudes of fame.

I'm not much of a diva anyway. Second children aren't good divas. My older sister claimed that role early on. As the conciliator and clown of the family, I had to cede it. But I had other tactics—like my bloody pinches or answering the phone and screaming to my older sister, *It's a boy!*—as if he were the first one who ever called her. I'm no saint. I just have other strategies—often verbal. I kill my enemies with words.

Doing the diva hardly appeals to me. But I once saw the opera singer Regina Resnik do it in Venice and I was full of awe.

"Watch me do the diva," she said as we swanned into the RAI studios in Palazzo Labia (I wish I could live in a palazzo with that name!). We wanted to screen her excellent movie on the Ghetto of Venice and needed a screening room. She managed to get the favor while convincing the head of Venetian RAI that she was doing *him* a favor.

Ever since then I have longed to be able to do the diva on appropriate occasions, but I'm too short.

As for the care and feeding of studs, I did that in my thirties and forties and had my fill. Every woman should try it briefly. Just don't give them your credit cards—or a car.

II.

ALTERED STATES, ENCHANTED PLACES, BOOZE *and the* MUSE

There were always far horizons that were more golden, bluer skies somewhere.

F. SCOTT FITZGERALD

When I was fourteen and at the height of my adoration for writers, I went alone to the 92nd Street Y to hear Dorothy Parker. Her stories and poems were alive for me, so I had no idea they had mostly been written more than thirty years earlier. She took a long time to come to the stage. The crowd grew fidgety. When she did appear—a little dumpling-shaped woman in her sixth or seventh decade—she was short for the podium and had a hard time finding the mike. Then she began to read in mumbles punctuated by long pauses. Her voice was nearly gone and clearly she was drunk. It was impossible to understand anything she was saying. I was so disappointed as I sat there clutching my copy of *The Best of Dorothy Parker,* which I had hoped to have autographed by my idol. Now I didn't *want* her autograph. Whenever my drinking demon starts to get the better of me, I think of her. I don't want to be her. Alcohol was the subtext of her unhappiness.

Probably she thought it was the cure.

I have given up alcohol for years at a time and then drifted back to it. I don't smoke dope. I never tried cocaine. I don't like gin or vodka or whiskey—martinis deliver a blow to the back of my head—but wine is one of the delights of life. I know good wine and can taste it. I won't drink plonk.

For this, the AA people mistrust me. I mistrust myself. Total abstinence is the only thing AA allows. I have often stood up at meetings and said, "My name's Erica and I'm an alcoholic." There is only one narrative: *I was a mess, I found AA, I am abstinent and now my life is radiant and God-filled. I can help you do the same.*

This program has saved the lives of many people I love and I am grateful to it. It saved my daughter's life! How can I fail to love it? *It works if you work it,* as we say at the close of meetings. I have been to many, many,

many meetings. And mostly, I find them inspiring. I'm not even sure why. When you describe a meeting to a friend—or even to yourself—it sounds silly. All kinds of people—young and old, rich and poor—sitting together to be strong, to be humble, to be utterly happy in the love and protection of God—*as you understand her.*

AA people are wonderful and kind. They believe in service and they give it. They are generous with their time. They are forgiving. If you drink again and come back, they always love and accept you. They are extraordinary. I wish Dorothy Parker had found them. She was so depressed and much of her depression, I'm convinced, was worsened by alcohol.

Of course she lived in a time when everyone drank to excess. Drunks populated the famed Algonquin Round Table. They thought it was necessary then to drink in order to be a writer. And many of them died of alcoholism and never wrote their best, most mature books. They were constantly soused, like Parker.

Think of the wreckage of lives of that and the previous (and following) generations: F. Scott Fitzgerald dying young, Faulkner drunker and drunker, Cheever struggling with the bottle all his writing life and finally getting sober at the bitter end—only to die of cancer. He wrote two marvelous books sober: *Falconer* and *Oh*

What a Paradise It Seems. But he also wrote pretty damn well when he was intermittently drunk—though he was more depressed. That is the joke of alcohol. We depressives are drawn to it for self-medication, but then it only makes us *more* depressed.

I feel wonderful when I'm abstinent, working out, eating vegetables and drinking tons of water and herbal tea—as at my favorite spa, Rancho La Puerta, in the desert of Baja California. But when I go to Provence or Umbria or Venice or Sicily, it seems criminal not to have a glass of wine. I have been abstinent in Provence, drinking bubbly water and Coca Light and looking longingly at those drinking Gigondas. I have been sober in Milan, sitting next to Umberto Eco (after La Milanesiana— the arts and literature festival where we both read our work). Umberto was happily guzzling some lovely wine from Tuscany. I studied the label, I poured for everyone else. I drank San Pellegrino water. But why? Would a glass have killed me? I was deep into abstinence then and I thought so.

Last summer, I was in Aspen with my dearest friend in the world, Gerri, and I remember an AA meeting where a woman in her seventies was beating herself up for having had *one sip* of wine on a trip to Paris with her friends.

"Why did I *do* it? Why am I *still* so self-destructive?" she mumbled moodily.

Because you were in Paris, I wanted to say. And the wine was amazing. But of course I couldn't say it. I was in the AA narrative: abstinence followed by illumination. No wine allowed—not even a sip.

Is this the only way not to destroy yourself like Parker did? I don't know. Some people are trying what they call "harm reduction," but the AA people hate them. I've been to "harm reduction" groups too. The therapist tries to get the group to reduce their intake of harmful substances, but she does not forbid them because she knows this sets up a rebellion within.

I know that when I was young I was horribly self-destructive. I drank margaritas then—not wine—till I passed out. I smoked anything you handed me and even took little blue pills, having no idea what they were. Those mysterious pills nearly killed me. If it hadn't been for two physicians at the party who walked me up and down and spooned coffee down my gullet, I might be dead. I have also passed out at parties from too much wine coupled with terror of the famous company. Once I was seated next to Robert Redford at a flashy New York dinner party and I was so scared by his good looks and his possible interest in me that I kept drinking wine till I passed out. I didn't get a date with Redford, and not only was I not invited back but my hosts gleefully told the gossip columns. Hardly kind of them. But even elegant people can stoop low. I got sober after that—and stayed sober a good long time. I even dated sober and had sex sober during my single days. Not an easy thing to manage.

Then I met Ken, who hardly drinks (his substance is food), and he said, "Why do you think you're an alcoholic?"

"Because I passed out at a party in front of Robert Redford, because I once nearly died from little blue pills mixed with margaritas, because I can't drink—that's why."

And he respected this, admired it, even wanted to go to meetings with me. He learned the jargon—he who tastes one sip of good wine and stops—even though he passed the Chevalier du Tastevin course (a really pretentious accreditation in wine tasting). He even gave me his silver Tastevin cup. He learned to call it "The Program" instead of AA. He learned about anonymity. He learned to say "It works if you work it" and "Let go, let God," and even "Meeting-makers make it." He is totally respectful of those who don't drink, and orders them

water or Coke or orange juice without blinking. He
never asks why.

As I felt more and more secure with him and more
and more relaxed, more and more cared for, I had a glass
of wine. (This was more than sixteen years ago.) We
were falling in love. We were reading each other poetry. I
was writing poetry for him. We were reciting old Omar
(the eleventh-century Persian poet and astronomer, as
interpreted by Edward Fitzgerald in 1859). Surely we
were reciting the verses out of order, but who cared?

> *Come, fill the Cup, and in the Fire of Spring*
> *The Winter Garment of Repentance fling:*
> *The Bird of Time has but a little way*
> *To fly—and Lo! The Bird is on the Wing.*
>
> *. . .*
>
> *Every morn I decide to repent at night*
> *For embracing the joys of heart and sight*
> *Yet every night, what seems right*
> *With all my might, embrace delight.*
>
> *. . .*
>
> *And if the Wine you drink, the Lip you press,*
> *End in the Nothing all Things end in—Yes—*
> *Then fancy while Thou art, Thou art but what*

Thou shalt be—Nothing—Thou shalt not be less.

. . .

Ah! my Beloved, fill the Cup that clears
To-day of past Regrets and future Fears—
To-morrow?—Why, To-morrow I may be
Myself with Yesterday's Sev'n Thousand Years.

You cannot quote Omar and drink Diet Coke. You cannot quote Omar and drink San Pellegrino. Wine is demanded. Wine is essential. You cannot be in love and not drink wine. Or I can't, anyway.

So it began. And I was moderate in my usage of wine. Older and wiser and married to my best friend, my soul mate, my darling, I drank with moderation and enjoyed it.

At that point, Molly was eleven. She turned twelve, thirteen, fourteen—those hellish years when mothers and daughters both go mad. She was in rebellion about my new marriage.

She wanted to be first in my life and Ken did too. Impossible. They tore me limb from limb at the breakfast table. He wanted me. She wanted me. I felt like a medieval martyr torn apart by wild horses.

But then I began to notice that they did this little act for *me*. When I went away to give a lecture or promote a book, they got along fine. I decided not to react and see what happened. Five years into the marriage, they were pals. He became the steady father she needed. And she became his daughter of the heart.

They formed a conspiracy to make fun of my absent-mindedness, my dreaminess, my constant dieting, my tendency to spend fortunes on clothes. They bonded. And I was happy. We'd become a family. We even took vacations with Ken's other stepdaughter, Samantha—and almost got along. It was tough, but it was worth it. Stepfamilies always take a lot of work.

Now Molly was sixteen, seventeen, and doing a lot of drugs. Some of them I'd never even heard of—like Ecstasy. They didn't exist in my day. And the pot was lethal, a hallucinogen overbred to be stronger than anything anyone *ever* smoked in the sixties—or seventies. She'd stop for a while and burn all the dealers' numbers, but then she'd start again. Like most parents, I didn't want to know. But I knew. I knew something was very wrong. She graduated from Riverdale Country School and began Wesleyan. I knew when I visited her in a dorm room with a sticky floor and a rug you could have smoked to get high that she was miserable. I knew she was lonely. I knew she was at risk.

Colleges stopped being in loco parentis in the sixties.

But the kids are not really mature enough to go away without any guidance, without parents, without friends. Molly was in bad shape and I didn't know the full extent of the cause. She wanted to come home and see her shrink. I agreed. She was better off home.

For a while she continued with a shrink who couldn't even figure out she was using. Of course she had contempt for him, as she later had contempt for a woman shrink who had no idea what was going on.

She applied to Barnard, my alma mater, and began school again. She went back to painting, for which she has a great gift. She worked in a gallery in SoHo and learned a lot about the art biz. But still she was miserable and going with a married guy.

Eventually she took a leave from Barnard too and worked at the Holly Solomon Gallery. And made various druggy friends in the art world.

The shit hit the fan when she was nineteen and had transferred to NYU. She was now, thank God, with a shrink who understood addiction.

One day she came to me and said:

"Mom, help me. I can't stop using coke. I think I'm going to die."

Her complexion was greenish, her hair bright auburn, her hands shaking, My first thought was to say, "It can't be that bad," but something stopped me. I didn't want to believe my daughter was a drug addict—what mother does? But I realized that both our lives might depend on my believing her. I was not totally innocent about her drug use, but I didn't want to believe how far it had gone.

"Tell me about it."

"Mom—I thought I could control it, I really thought I could, but I keep wanting more. I stay up all night and then take downers to come down. I'm afraid I'll be one of those people who never wakes up. I'm turning into a coke whore. You have no idea how easy it is to be a coke whore in New York."

My daughter is a drama queen but somehow I believed her this time. I could see from the greenish color of her skin that she was telling the truth.

"What do you want to do?"

"I think I need to go to rehab. I really do. It terrifies me. I'll lose my job at Holly's. But otherwise I think I'll lose my life."

I hold her in my arms smelling the sour smell of cigarette tobacco and vomit. I remember her baby smell, her sweet head smelling of baby oil, her sweet tush smelling of baby crap. How can your children get so far away from where they started?

I immediately start making phone calls. By that night, Molly and I are on a plane for Minnesota.

Even though it's November, it's midwinter in Minnesota. It's always midwinter in Minnesota. We are standing in baggage claim when a chubby woman in a parka comes up to us.

"Molly?" she says.

"I'm Erica, this is Molly."

"I'm your transportation," she says. "I'm Mary M."

We get into a station wagon and drive north. It starts snowing. I hold Molly's hand.

"I'm scared, Mom."

"No reason to be scared," says Mary calmly, "the worst is behind you."

About two hours north of the airport, we arrive at a group of brick buildings in the wilderness. There is a frozen lake, tall pine trees, fields of snow.

Getting out of the car, I see that my breath is making puffs of smoke in the night air. Molly and I are led into an office where a short black man with a clipboard has some questions for us. We fill out papers, sign releases.

"I need to talk to Molly alone now," he says. "Probably you should wait outside."

"Don't go, Mom."

"I think I should."

"Molly," says the man, a counselor called Jim R., "I need to ask you some specific history of what brought you here and I think you might be more comfortable talking if your mother isn't here."

"O.K.," she says.

I wait outside in a cubicle, muttering prayers under my breath. I am full of remorse. How could I have let this kid go away to college? How could I have missed all this? How could I have been so immersed in my own problems?

Molly stays with Jim R. an hour or so while my mind races. Then she comes out, her eyes red, her nose running. Jim and I walk her down the hall to Detox and again there are papers to sign. Molly is taken into a little room with a bed and a sink. A nurse comes in and searches her luggage.

"Why don't you get some sleep?" she says. "We'll take good care of her."

"Go, Mom, I'll be O.K., I promise."

And I am escorted down a long underground corridor until we come to another building. Upstairs, a locked door and a series of rooms along a hall. One of these rooms is mine. It has two narrow beds bolted to the floor, a few Spartan tables and lamps. The bathroom has a paper bath mat and two tiny white towels. I shed my clothes and crawl into the narrow bed. I am shaking.

"God help me," I mutter. "God, please be there, please."

There have been lots of times in my life when I felt I had hit bottom, but this was the lowest. Molly was my future, all the dreams I had not fulfilled—like having a son, having movies made of my work, being the success in show business my father had always wanted to be or me to be for him. I needed Molly to live far more than I needed to live myself.

When I wake up at five in the morning, I find my room looks out on the frozen lake. Little huts are set up on the ice. Small bundled figures are walking across, leaving tracks in the snow. It is the quietest place I have ever been. You can listen to your thoughts here. Minnesota—I love you.

I quickly dress—my city clothes are all wrong, of course—and walk outside in the snow. My thin shoes crunch and I can feel the cold straight through. Still, I find a path through the tall firs and I follow it as long as I can stand the cold. Then I reverse direction and come back.

In one of the lounges of the building where my room is, I find a fire going in a stone fireplace and coffee and donuts laid out. I get some coffee and drink it in front of the fire. I pick up a book called *Serenity* from one of the tables. Here are the words I open to: "When we stop thinking of fears and doubts, they begin to lose their power. When we stop believing good things are impossible, anything becomes possible."

The rehab had no phones and my cell phone didn't work. I couldn't call anyone. This was a blessing. I could think. Thinking is well nigh impossible in our multitasking world. Thinking is good. So is prayer.

After a month in Minnesota, Molly came home sober. I stopped drinking again. I needed to support her and I needed total clarity. Ken supported me in this too. He loved me sober or not.

Her story is not really mine to tell. She has told it from her point of view in *Normal Girl*. The mother's point of view and the daughter's converge only occasionally. She will see it differently as her son Maxi grows up and as she grows up more and I grow older.

Perspectives always shift as we age. Thank God for that too.

I have been trying to understand addiction and creative people. Why are we so prone to it?

. . .

In order to create something that didn't exist before, it's necessary to go into a state where dream and reality are equally available and where time does not exist. Some psychologists refer to this as the "flow state." It was best defined for me by an unpronounceable writer named Mihaly Csikszentmihalyi in an excellent book called *Flow: The Psychology of Optimal Experience.* Optimal experience, or the flow state, is characterized by the suspension of the sense of time, the obliteration of self-consciousness and the feeling that we are doing something for its own sake and not for its outcome. This is a perfect description of writing, or sex, or sailing, or ballet dancing or painting or musical composition, or . . . you fill in the blanks. Athletes breaking records are in flow. So are writers writing, dancers dancing, sailors sailing. Immersed in their craft, they find flow— which is its own reward. We awaken from it refreshed and happy, as after a long vacation or an ecstatic dream. The universe seems harmonious. We are doing what we are meant to do within it. We are in tune with the world and ourselves.

I usually find flow only early in the morning when I

am scarcely out of the dream world and there are likely to be no interruptions. I like to write before the day begins for other people. The hours between 4 a.m. and 9 a.m. are sacrosanct. I often inhabit them while finishing a book. More often, I work between 8 a.m. and 1 p.m. I get more done in those five hours than in a whole day of starts and stops.

Because the flow of writing is so pleasurable when it's working, it's not surprising that mind-altering drugs tempt writers. We hope to continue the flow state by artificial means—drugs, alcohol—and in the beginning it seems to work. At least it banishes the inner censor for a while and frees up the hand that moves over the page.

But the wrecked lives of alcoholic American writers testify to the strength of the attraction to alcohol and the way it backfires. Apparently, it's so painful to make something out of nothing that people never stop hoping for the magic potion.

In his book *The Varieties of Religious Experience,* William James (brother of Henry and Alice) talks about mystical states and their connection to mind-altering drugs. Mystical states, says James, have a noetic quality. Those who experience them believe they are gaining knowledge by blurring the intellect:

They are states of insight into depths of truth unplumbed by the discursive intellect. They are illuminations, revelations, full of significance and importance, all inarticulate though they remain.

James believed that these mystical states, though alcohol or drugs may heighten them, are necessarily fleeting. Sometimes they take the form of déjà vu experiences ("of having 'been here before'"); sometimes they take the form of a vision of God or of God's angelic messengers.

We can also access these states through staring at the sea and listening to its roar, through chanting or fasting or wandering in the wilderness for forty days. These things take a lot more discipline than the instantaneous pleasure of a joint or a glass of wine. Mystics tell us that reaching the flow state without chemicals is better than being drunk or stoned, but most of us are not mystics. The quick fix appeals to us. At first it seems to deliver easy ecstasy. Only after a while do most of us realize that blurring the censor through drugs and alcohol also blurs the mind. At first we think we write better this way, but although the feeling is fiercely intense the writing deteriorates. The purpose of writing is to see things as they are, to see the world more clearly and to rejoice in this clarity of vision.

We look for spiritual transcendence in mind-altering drugs, and for a time it seems to be found there. And then it's gone. And in its place is depression and fear. I have found through long, excruciating experience that for me the most enduring transcendence is found in the trance of writing.

The key is probably moderation, but I have never been good at moderation. I am always hoping I will learn it so I can access the ecstasy without letting it devour me. One of my novels, *Any Woman's Blues,* chronicles this struggle through the life of a painter called Leila Sand. Leila hates the jargon of AA, but she finds herself mysteriously helped by it. She drags her addict lover, Dart (the character inspired by the meat van man), into sobriety, but when he falls off the wagon she decides to let him go and stay herself. Through this alter ego, I tried to make sense of my own attraction to mystical states, my own longing for moderation and my own addictive behavior. I wrote about the connection between addictive sex and addictive substances, the connection between mystical ecstasy and ecstatic sex, how they both come from the *more* demon. Writing the novel did help me begin to understand and exorcize my own addictions. Leila was a version of myself through whose struggles against addiction I could comprehend my own inner battles.

In recent years, there have been many books about the struggle for sobriety. Some of them are thoughtful. Others use the experiences of drink and drugs for special unearned effects.

Sometimes it seems that as soon as someone brags about recovery, she falls off the wagon immediately. No sooner does a celebrity boast of the wonders of rehab on the cover of *People* than that celebrity gets arrested for drunk driving. Better not to talk too publicly of cures. Better to fight one's own battles privately. It may be bad luck to gloat about recovery—which is why I will never write that I've recovered. There are so many ways to self-destruct with addiction—shopping, eating, gambling, going into debt. The whole American economy would collapse if we all recovered.

The first time I got drunk I was fifteen and I drank fifteen screwdrivers—just a year after I saw Dorothy Parker and vowed never to drink. It was on my parents' twenty-fifth wedding anniversary at their apartment on Central

Park West. A picture of me exists from that party. I am falling out of my black strapless gown, my long blond hair shadows my eyes and I look like I just saw a vision of paradise. Probably that's one of the few times I ever saw paradise while drunk—though I was always looking for it.

My parents were of the generation that associated champagne with a good time—and when they got really prosperous after World War II, they delighted in buying cases of good champagne for their friends.

"I love to eat! I love to drink! I love to fuck!" I remember one of their arty friends shouting, as she stripped off her sheer blouse at one of their parties. Was I shocked? Not really, but I retreated upstairs to hide behind a book, as usual. My parents' parties always had a raffish, bohemian flair—even after they acquired the accoutrements of bourgeois success. Drinking just went with being creative and flush. Nobody thought there was anything wrong with being drunk. But celebratory drinking is entirely different from the drinking we do in search of ecstasy. The door into the unconscious has to be pried open somehow, and we always think alcohol will facilitate that. For a while it does and then it may well slam shut. I often think of alcohol as a genie in a bottle. It promises everything but eventually imprisons you in the bottle itself. You write with great freedom but in the morning discover only gobbledygook. You finally admit that Shakespeare is a better poet than Drunkspeare.

I try to make my love of good wine jibe with my understanding of the genie in the bottle. I never write after a glass of wine.

The people who can drink moderately don't have this problem, but they are probably not seekers of ecstasy, either. People who most crave ecstasy are probably least capable of moderation. I long to be proven wrong about this.

Blake says: *The road of excess leads to the palace of wisdom*. But what if you die on that road? Is that the wisdom you were meant to have? Is death the final revelation? The Polish Jews waiting for the Holocaust at the end of Isaac Bashevis Singer's great novel *The Family Moskat* tell each other sadly that perhaps death is the only Messiah they can hope for.

The number of writers who have chronicled the sorrows of gin is great, but for me John Cheever transcends them all. The darkness of *The Journals of John Cheever* is very much the darkness of the struggle with alcohol. I know of no book that makes alcohol less appealing. And yet the protagonist of these journals has to learn this over and over. "The battle with booze goes on. I weed the chrysanthemums and hold away from the bottle until half past eleven but not a second longer."

What is Cheever looking for? "What he would have liked, what he dreamed of, was some elixir, some magical, brightly colored pill that would put the spring back in his step, the gleam in his eye, the joy of life in his heart."

The magic elixir seems to be a cure for depression. And there is no doubt that alcohol abuse and depression are connected. At first, alcohol seems to take off the depressive edge and bring that spring to the step, but, since it's a depressant, for many people it only ends by making depression worse. This is hard to see in yourself because the substance changes its effects over time.

Stephen King has a very honest account of his own alcoholism in *On Writing*. He even sees his novel *Misery* as a struggle with addiction. He acknowledges that the marriage between alcoholism and creative endeavor "is one of the great pop-intellectual myths of our time." Writers like Hemingway, Fitzgerald and Sherwood Anderson unwittingly romanticized alcoholism. But if you read the biographies of these writers you will see that alcohol cut short their creative lives—as it did Edna

St. Vincent Millay's and Dylan Thomas's. The search for the elixir, the search for relief from depression, becomes a search for the death of consciousness. I think we are ready for some new myths. But if the devil has the best tunes and the angels bore us with their unending serenity, how shall we find them? Destruction always makes a better story than perfection. Perfection usually makes us feel we are being lectured.

The question remains: How to pierce the veil of the unconscious? Better than the elixir is ritual or routine. Sometimes I start the day writing nonsense until it turns into sense. I scribble, never lifting the pen from the page and never giving in to self-criticism. I knock my mother and grandmother off my shoulder. This is a kind of automatic writing, which puts me in touch with my unconscious and what it needs to tell me. It is a sort of dreaming on paper. I do it better on a yellow legal pad with a fast-flowing pen than on the computer, where writing looks too much like print.

Meditation sometimes works (the best mantra I have found is: *No thought, no thought, no thought*), as does playing music, or reading poetry, taking a walk or a swim. When all else fails, there's prayer. As Thomas Merton says in *New Seeds of Contemplation,* "It is not we who choose to awaken ourselves, but God who chooses to awaken us."

The notion of God brings us to the muse—the male writer's form of the demon. The muse also embodies creativity. She's fickle. She appears and disappears at will. We can't control her. And because we can't control her, we hate her as much as we love her. We try to summon her with sex, with falling in love, with mind-altering drugs. But the fact is, she won't be summoned. She alights when it damn well pleases her. She falls in love with one artist, then deserts him for another. She's a real bitch.

For me anyway, the muse takes the form of the demon lover—the one Singer wrote about. He appears at dusk and is banished by dawn. He is part vampire. We long for him to come and drink our blood.

Let me show you the fang marks on my throat.

Of course, the muse or demon lover is an aspect of self. I know damn well that when I am summoning this creature, I am really trying to connect with the part of myself that is free, imaginative and able to fly. This part of myself often gets lost under familial obligations and duties. I objectify my imagination as a separate creature, knowing this is metaphor. The muse or demon lover is inside me. I have to release the inhibitions that imprison me. I have to get rid of the voices that urge: *Write nice things, don't embarrass the family; remember the plight of the Jews; and be sure to write good things about Israel.* . . . Nothing freezes the imagination like family loyalty or political correctness.

What we all live for, hope for, would die for is what Henry Miller calls "the dictation." That's when the words take off on a frolic of their own, when you don't seem to be writing or thinking but rather taking down some divine dictation. When Miller said, "A writer shouldn't think much," he meant that we are better off tapping into the dictation than thinking about it. But the problem is that the dictation comes so seldom. Sometimes you wait and wait and wait for it and it seems like it will never come again. And sometimes it doesn't.

We can't dismiss the fact that for most of human history, we've been flirting with various modes of intoxication—whether for religious ecstasy or erotic. I'm convinced that a lot of our flirtation with drink, drugs and mind-altering love affairs is an attempt to summon the dictation. We want to get to Xanadu on the express train, but Coleridge's person from Porlock keeps on

blocking our way. (Coleridge tells the story of compos-
ing a great poem in a dream but losing it to a knock on
the door from a mysterious "person from Porlock.")

In my dreams, I am often climbing stairs or trying to
get to airports or train stations, but my luggage impedes
my progress. I attempt to hitch rides with strangers who
take me far out of my way and lose my luggage. Sometimes my dreams resemble Escher stairs that lead up and
down but go nowhere. I look down and there are galax-
ies below me. At times I dream that I have written an
amazing book, dictated by the demon, a book far better
than any I could have written awake. All my mentors
praise it, and when I wake up, it's gone. My deepest wish
is to find that book.

A dream:

*I am digging just to the left of my house in Con-
necticut. What am I digging for? The novel I buried
several years ago that I now want back. It's buried in
three places—manuscripts wrapped in plastic, then
burlap—consisting of worksheets and two drafts. I
find the worksheets, but the other two manuscripts
are gone and the neighbors are trying to stop me
from digging because they claim the land is theirs.
The ground has just been covered with new slates as*

a patio. I must dig to get my work back, but they forbid me. I am desperate. I must have those drafts! How will I do it? Dig when no one is looking? Dig at night? I am really upset. How could I have stupidly buried those pages in what turned out to be a public area? I thought it was private.

The dream couldn't be more obvious—at least to me. The three are the three sisters of whom I am the middle, the meat in the sandwich, the tale-teller. The book is my novel-in-progress—which I've buried and reburied for the last five years (though in the dream, to disguise it, it seems to be *Sappho's Leap*). The dream is my way of telling myself, Get going already! You can't live forever. This book seems to be the necessary link to the next. It is taking me there by revealing my self-deceptions. It's also telling me I can't write unless I'm willing to unbury the dead.

In my dreams, often I am writing what Henry Miller, in his *Paris Review* interview, called "cadenzas":

The passages I refer to are tumultuous, the words fall over one another. I could go on indefinitely. Of course I think that is the way one should write all the time. You see here the whole difference, the great dif-

ference, between Western and Eastern thinking and behavior and discipline. If, say, a Zen artist is going to do something, he's had a long preparation of discipline and meditation, deep quiet thought about it and then no thought, silence, emptiness and so on— it might be for months, it might be for years. Then, when he begins, it's like lightning, just what he wants—it's perfect. Well, this is the way all art should be done. But who does it? We all lead lives that are contrary to our profession.

So I live with a ravine between my wishes and reality. Most days I sit at the machine or the yellow pad, doodling and feeling like an abject failure. Ecstasy eludes me. Even clarity and simplicity elude me. Then one day the cadenzas come. But they only come because of the days of doodling.

I know a writer who writes two books a year, drives a Rolls, has several yachts and planes and houses and lives like a WASP rajah.

"How do you write so fast?" I ask him.

"By lowering my standards. You could write faster if you lowered your standards too."

Maybe this is true, maybe his attempt at a joke, but I have no interest in reading his books. I only want his freedom from economic insecurity. Yet many people *do* read his books. They devour them like candy. And probably don't remember them. But in the depths of my envious heart, I tell myself I wish I could lower my standards. But then I catch myself. I am lying to myself again.

I am doing the best I can—and so, probably, is he. I could write faster, but the books would suck. Plus, this guy has a formula that works. Formulas are a gift. I don't disparage the ability to entertain. But I will never be that kind of writer. Katherine Anne Porter said, "I look upon literature as an art, and I believe that if you misuse it or abuse it, it will leave you. It is not a thing you can nail down and use as you want. You have to let it use you, too."

Waiting for the dictation (*la dictée,* as in French class) is one of the ways in which it uses me. There are thousands of other ways. I have to humble myself for the demon to come at all—no matter how many Rolls-Royces, yachts or planes I promise him. Why should a demon care about cars or yachts or planes when he has his own wings?

.   .   .

The first time I came to Venice as an adult, it was after a trip to Russia, then the Soviet Union. The Soviet trip was purgatorial, as Soviet trips tended to be in those days. It was a literary junket organized by the late Harrison Salisbury. Robert Bly, Gwendolyn Brooks, Susan Sontag, Studs and Ida Turkel, Irving and Jean Stone, Arthur and Alexandra Schlesinger, Harrison and his wife, Charlotte, were the American guests.

Harrison, who was a one-man cultural exchange maven, invited us to meet our Soviet counterparts and tour the parts of the country we especially wanted to see. Yevgeny Yevtushenko and Andrey Voznesensky were promised, among others.

The wonderful Chicago poet Gwendolyn Brooks and I shared a double-decker sleeping compartment from Moscow to Kiev, but we didn't sleep. We stayed up all night talking about poetry or reciting it to each other. Robert Bly wandered from compartment to compartment, playing his balalaika.

When we arrived in Kiev, we were paired up with our translators, who were clearly also reporting to some lowly apparatchik at the KBG about everything we said and did. That was also standard in 1983.

Matrons in black guarded each floor of the hotel and impounded our keys and passports.

For most of the day we sat in meetings wearing head-phones in which we could listen to endless droning speeches in Russian or English. Every hour or so we were summoned into the hallway for frozen shots of vodka, which I guzzled (not abstaining then), and gray greasy beluga in buds of butter, which we perched on toasted pumpernickel crescents or ate with spoons of abalone shell. What beluga it was! Could Marx have known that the best beluga would be reserved for Party members and their guests?

At lunchtime, there was another three-hour food orgy with more beluga caviar, borscht, mystery meat and icy vodka. For dessert, there were pastries and sweet Georgian champagne.

Susan Sontag, who was nothing if not pragmatic about her career, toasted "the kitchen staff that prepared the meal." Clearly she had been here before and understood the full spectrum of appropriate Communist behavior.

Only at night, when the vodka flowed even more freely, did my sloe-eyed translator break down and weep.

"Soviet Union no good place for womens," she whispered. "Men drink too much wodka, become *why-o-lent*."

Studs Turkel would roam the city with his tape re-

corder trying to collect impressions of life under Communism, but an overenthusiastic comrade confiscated his machine.

During a performance of the opera *The Bartered Bride,* my translator lushly whispered to me, "Dat is fate of all Russian womens!"

The sense of being constantly spied on, the compulsory toasts, the never-ending drunkenness got to me quickly. It was a country I couldn't wait to leave but was afraid would never release me. I went to Odessa in search of my Russian relatives but never found any—even with my translator's help. I assumed my mother's family, the Mirskys, had perished in pogroms or fallen into a ravine in Babi Yar or emigrated. Jews of my grandparents' generation couldn't wait to get out of Russia. My grandfather left twice—once at fourteen, once at sixteen. The first time, he was captured crossing the border and was sent to the tiny town of his birth, where he knew no one. Two years later, he made another run for it and wound up in Paris, where all young artists wanted to go.

"If I'd been killed in the Manchurian war, you wouldn't exist!"

I was six, and when I tried to think of not existing I couldn't.

At the Moscow airport, where we spent hours having

our exit papers shuffled, I panicked and was certain I'd never get away. The Soviet apparatchiks would keep me there for various dreamlike Kafkaesque crimes. I would never see my dear daughter or Dart of the curved cock again. I would be tried for the sins of my grandfather Mirsky, who escaped the draft and wound up in Paris, living as an art student on bananas donated by a shadowy French Rothschild.

Arriving in Venice from Moscow was like escaping to Shangri-La. The pool at the Cipriani was a magical baptism, restoring your right to be free (and bankrupt). Venice was freedom itself. Whatever restriction there was in the stone city was washed away in the reflected one. The doubleness of Venice and its reflection left room for everything.

Dart and I wallowed in luxury at the Cipriani—and damn the cost (all on my tab). We stayed in bed all day, ordering up room service between frenzied bouts of lovemaking and wandered the streets all night. I thought I knew Venice as a city of sex and opulence, but it would take twenty more years before I *really* knew Venice. I would have to visit it with friends and alone, with lovers and bereft, in shabby houses and elegant hotels, before I had any idea of what Venice meant in my life.

Venice was my touchstone. For years, I went back there to finish each of my books. And each time Venice was different. Or was it? Was the city merely a screen onto which I projected myself?

Both my demons and angels accosted me in Venice, but often they changed places so that you hardly knew who was who. Sometimes the city held me bewitched by its beauty. Other times, I couldn't wait to flee. Venice is an island—gossipy, claustrophobic and haunted. The people who live there all the time are ravenous for new blood to slake their boredom with each other. They fall upon the newcomer like vampires.

I lived in Venice on and off for several years in order to write *Shylock's Daughter*.

Certain books must be written among the spirits that summoned them. Could Mary Shelley have written *Frankenstein* except far from England in a chalet on Lake Geneva that all its laudanum-laced inhabitants believed to be haunted? Could Byron have written *Don Juan* except in Venice?

I remember working on my Venetian novel in a friend's house in Venice, where my room overlooked a small canal whose water threw shimmering reflections on the ceiling. I've always found my dreams are richer in

Venice, and every time I slept I awoke with more incidents for the novel. I'm sure that book could not have been written anywhere else.

Arriving in Venice, I am always thrilled by its magnificence and I am convinced I want to live in Venice forever. After a few weeks, the feeling fades. I feel trapped by my watery second home and must escape to terra firma. It is the doubleness of the place that makes it both alluring and repellent. Time stands still in Venice, but do we want time to stand still?

I used to go to Venice searching for my demon. I thought that if I found the magic place, my life would turn magical and my writing would fly beyond the limitations every writer knows.

All through the eighties I rented houses in Venice. The first was in Salute (behind the Church of Santa Maria della Salute), the last on Giudecca—near the Santa Eufemia vaporetto stop. I would decamp from New York when Molly's school was done in June and return when it resumed in September. The most memorable of these rented places was a decaying sixteenth-century palazzo my visiting friends called "Palazzo Erica" (not its real name). It was one of a row of palazzi facing Venice from Giudecca. Near Harry's Dolci and the *traghetto* to the

Zattere, a brisk walk from the Cipriani pool (where I swam in the afternoon), it had been owned by a retired art historian from the Metropolitan Museum of Art who hadn't the cash to restore it. Since she had no children, she left it, when she died of cancer, to two of her protégés who hadn't the cash to restore it either.

I was one of various renters. The "house" consisted of the *piano nobile* (four bedrooms, a *salotto*, a library filled with wonderful books about the history of art), a kitchen with a skylight that leaked copiously in rainstorms, a neglected rose garden with one hugely prolific pear tree in the middle and a dark but totally separate studio apartment on the ground floor with a bar and sofa bed, where I met my gorgeous but wholly unreliable Venetian lover most mornings while Molly and her nanny, Margaret, were out shopping. That was in my single days.

Leonello had a grace that all Don Juans might envy. His manners were perfect. His maneuvering of his *motoscafo* in and out of difficult docks was an art. His dancing presaged the grace of his fucking. And he was a slow seducer, slow to bed and slow to finish. He was of medium height, with eyes the color of unfiltered Tuscan olive oil, curly salt-and-pepper hair, golden skin and not a word of English besides "O.K." In Italian, everything is sexier, and I owe whatever conversational skills I have to him—though most of them cannot be used out of bed.

"Palazzo Erica" was surely haunted. Elizabeth Gardner, the art historian who had come to die in Venice, was padding around her house—coaching me in art history—as were dozens of ghosts from other eras. Some of the ghosts were friendly. Many were sex-obsessed. And some were sinister. Ghosts are just like the living. They come in all flavors. But ghosts are always good for writing.

I knew a cocktail pianist in Venice who said he was drawn back again and again by the deep feeling he had lived there in another life. One night he dreamed of being a sixteenth-century baker and woke up covered with flour. His landlady had told him that the ground floor where he slept had once been a bakery. Do I believe it? Maybe and maybe not. I believe *he* believed it. Venice does that to people.

Many people come to retire and die in Venice. Often when they come, they think they are coming to live. And then they sicken and die like Aschenbach in Thomas Mann's *Death in Venice*. That novella may be why I never bought a house in Venice but only rented. I was sure the city would capture me for one of its ghosts. It has that power.

Venice needs artists to die there and add to its myth. Think of Ezra Pound, Diaghilev, Mahler. . . . Venice is a ghoul, a sort of vampire—a very beautiful vampire, but beauty is one of a vampire's many snares. The famous artists usually stay buried in the verdant cemetery island of San Michele. The obscure ones are dug up and tossed on an obscure ossuary island—bones, teeth, hair. Even in death, fame is unforgiving.

Provence is also beautiful and the food is far better than the food in Venice. It has fascinating Roman ruins, like Glanum near Saint-Rémy, the Pont du Gard, the temples of Nîmes and the beautiful village perches of the Drôme. But though it is lovely beyond measure, it holds no deep attraction for me.

Venice generates dreams and daydreams too. Sleeping on water—whether in a boat or a city like a boat—floats your sane mind away.

Here is a dream:

I am having an affair with Bill Clinton with my husband's knowledge and approval. We are meeting in various places around New York City—including in a big old fifties convertible with rocket-shaped fenders of turquoise and silver. Bill and I are not very careful about not getting caught. My husband knows and seems not to mind. Hillary is our only worry. Nevertheless, we are more and more brazen. The sex is great, but I am getting nervous about exposure in the press. Bill is very nonchalant about concealing our connection.

Now Bill is taking me to a place I don't know up near Columbia. It is a high-rise for faculty on West 125th Street (Bill and Hillary are apparently both teaching at Columbia). When we arrive at the apartment, my first thought is about how scuzzy it is, how inappropriate for such important people. I wonder why Bill has brought me there if he shares it with his wife. Suddenly all these graduate students come into the living room, followed by Hillary, who is totally unperturbed, thinks I'm just another of Bill's students, has no idea I am Bill's lover.

"Let's go," says my husband, who is with me. We start to leave. I worry that I don't have Bill's phone number and therefore may never see him again. Don't worry, I tell myself. He has my number and will call me as he always does when he wants to see me. I can live with that. "But don't you mind his hav-

ing all the power?" a voice in my head asks. What
can I do about it? I say to myself philosophically. In
my heart I know he'll be back.

Fucking Bill Clinton? Well, I guess I'll have to stand in
line. I'm hardly the only one who finds him sexy. Even
after open-heart surgery, he has more life force than
most men of any age. Life force is the ultimate sex
appeal. I know that Bill Clinton's Achilles' heel is lusting
for flashy broads (his mother was a flashy broad and
men never get over their mothers). I wonder if I'm trashy
enough for him, but I can dream, can't I?

Maybe I can dress up like his dear dead mother, Virginia Kelley (when she was a babe in the forties)—or
Gennifer Flowers—or even poor betrayed Monica Le-
winsky. Men are pretty unsubtle creatures. I have been
involved with brilliant poets who liked me to wear tacky
underwear. Insisted on it, in fact. I have known fierce
intellectuals (who wrote for the *TLS* or *The New York
Review of Each Other's Books*) who could only get hard
staring at Frederick's of Hollywood crotchless panties.
So I know the drill. No wonder Monica snagged the not
impossible him with a thong—uncomfortable and chaf-
ing though they are. (They tend to give me diaper rash.)

But the point of the dream seems to be that I have to

give up control. I can't get in touch with Bill. He has to get in touch with me. My husband is cool about our affair, but Hillary has to be fooled and Bill is very nervous about her. She's a bossy dame, but he needs her.

He loves tawdry broads and flashy fifties cars. He's a boy straight outta *Grease*. He worships Elvis. But he chose to marry a girl out of Nancy Drew: a smart virgin who can figure out just about any crime—including his. She hasn't figured *us* out yet, but he fears she *will*. His wife knows full well that he's torn between trash and virginity, between dumb and smart, between hot and cool. He's my soul mate. I used to get excited by boys in black leather jackets on Harleys. I would never have married Mr. Motorcycle, but I sure liked to fuck him. In that, Bill and I are the same.

So what's the dream about? A lot of things. Giving up control. Nostalgia for the fifties. Nostalgia for my sex-filled days at Barnard and Columbia (we're on 125th Street, after all), nostalgia for my bad boys and Italian studs, nostalgia for my single life. I'm also back at school, learning again, and the former President is my teacher. But so is Hillary. I don't want to betray her, but she's married to my favorite political hunk. What a dilemma!

This is really an Oedipal dream. I love both Daddy

and Mother, but it's him I want to fuck. My parents were flirtatious—both of them. And we called them by their first names. My father was Seymour. He was handsome and hot. It was hard to think of him as my father. And he adored me. I always wanted him and sought him in stand-ins all over the world. Men who can play the piano and drums always turn me on.

And my mother. I called her Eda. She was my nemesis and my ego ideal all in one confusing package, like my dream Hillary. Once she actually accused me of being in love with my father.

"You're mad at me because you adore your father," she screamed, when I was fifteen and at my most hateful toward her. Of course she was right.

I could go on interpreting this dream forever. But the main thing, I think, is the loss of control. This man is the boss—my President!—and *I* always want to be the boss. I cannot control him. I have to wait for his calls.

If this book were a novel, I'd describe actually having an affair with a character like Bill Clinton. It would be an anguishing affair because he's a totally divided man. He's bonded to brainy Hillary, but he lusts in his heart for women like his mother. No wonder he drove Monica crazy. He would do the same to you or me.

Yet I can certainly imagine myself hanging around

Harlem in the hopes of seeing Bill Clinton. Or maybe I could stake him out in Westchester when Hillary's not around. Heart surgery or no heart surgery, the man's got to be restless by now. He's been good too long. Have I?

But the truth is that instead of stalking the ex-President, I'm hosting a fund-raiser for Hillary at my apartment in New York. I can dream, but I also have a sane mind.

So I go to Venice to dream. Everyone should have a special place to dream. "Poets have to dream and dreaming in America is no cinch," Saul Bellow said. I think what he meant by that was that America worships business and money and that these obsessions leave no place for dreams. When I think of all the American writers who escaped to Europe to write, I think Bellow was onto something. But maybe it's just a question of getting away from home. If Europe is home, you may have to flee to America to write.

Home and away. We all require a place that represents *away*. Even Venetians have to go away. Terra firma has a special lure when you live in Venice. Once a month, you cannot wait to get out of the miasma and back to the traffic.

These days, full-time Venetians argue about curing *acqua alta*. Sea level is rising and the ground floors of many Venetian buildings have been abandoned to the waters. Piazza San Marco can sometimes only be traversed on wooden platforms. Immense underwater sea gates have been proposed and begun and politicians argue about the cost of construction and whether these gates will make Venice even more of a museum than it already is. Ordinary people can't afford to live in Venice and the population is falling. Tourism is the only robust industry. A city where there is no industry but tourism grows cynical.

Part of the pathos and charm of Venice is its uselessness. It has been creating festivals devoted to its uselessness for nearly a thousand years. Venice exists as the epitome of *away*. Like the myth of Atlantis, it is kept alive by the human need for a far and magical place.

We would prefer that place to have turrets and minarets and gliding boats with curled prows, but really what we are looking for is transformation. The enchanted lands of fairy tales promise this transformation—Snow White awakened by the kiss of a prince, Hansel and Gretel defeating the evil witch, Dorothy realizing she can always go home. It seems we want to go to a magic place to find the seed of magic in ourselves.

"I stood in Venice, on the Bridge of Sighs," Byron wrote, "A palace and a prison on each hand: / I saw from out the wave her structures rise /As from the stroke of the enchanter's wand." The presence of that "enchanter" is the key to Venice. It seems to be a place where the imagination is unbound, where the creator can hear the whisperings of the muses in the soft susurration of the wavelets that lap against crumbling marble steps.

The sensible and driven Erica, who is her father's daughter, wants to flee as soon as possible.

III.

THE ITCHING *of a* SCAR, *or* NO BUSINESS LIKE SHOW BUSINESS

Yes; it is the dangerous hour of clear understanding. Oh for a kindly hand to tap at my door. Oh for a face to come between me and the made-up counselor spying on me out of the mirror! . . . I! Involuntarily, I glance at the mirror as I formulate the word. That certainly is myself, though unrecognizable in my make-up of red and mauve, which begins to melt. Shall I have to wait so long that my features will melt away too? Will nothing be left of my reflection but a tinted smudge trailing on the glass like a long murky tear?

COLETTE

My father always regretted leaving show business. He made a lot of money selling tchotchkes, but what he really respected were musicians, songwriters and composers. He was not a trained musician and he idolized them above all artists. He used to say the name "Juilliard" with the same reverence he reserved for Mozart, Brahms and Puccini. He knew what was good and he didn't measure up to his own standards.

He wrote a few published songs in the thirties, played

nightclubs and weddings as a bandleader, even introduced one great song in a Broadway show—"Begin the
Beguine." He'd auditioned for Cole Porter and got the
gig in *Jubilee* (1935). That was destined to be the high
point of his musical career. At an early age, I knew what
moved him—fame. I was not a musician, but I was
always comfortable on stage. I was a terrible ballet
dancer as a little girl, but when Tex and Jinx (the celebrated talk show hosts of the fifties) came to the American School of Ballet they picked me to be interviewed on
TV because I was such a fluent talker. Even now, I can
stand up in front of thousands of people and feel no fear,
but when I turn in a book manuscript I'm a wreck.

At camp I was no athlete but found a way to get attention anyway. I couldn't play softball and that was all
that mattered at the camp my benighted parents had
sent me to at age seven. The girls in my bunk hated me
for being a bookworm, a ball dropper and for speaking
with what they called "an English accent" because it
wasn't Brooklynese. (My mother was born in Britain and
still, at ninety-three, has certain Britishisms of speech.)
I was never so lonely and lost in my life.

When it came time to take the camp photo, we were all
herded into the "rec" room, where dozens of photos of
camp from years past lined the walls. In every photo there

were hundreds of identical blobs representing camper faces. Most were so small that the kid's identity was lost.

I studied these monuments to years past and some devilish daring rose up in me. When we had been carefully placed on benches and arranged according to height, when the photographer looked through the lens and instructed us to say "cheese," I suddenly whipped my head to one side to look different from the rest. In the middle of all these blobs would be a profile with a ponytail.

"You *rooned* the picture!" my fellow campers yelled.

I pretended contrition. I was secretly delighted to have "rooned" the picture. I believe that was the first stirring of my lust for fame. Not to blend in, not to be a blob, not to be invisible in an overcrowded world—these are some of the reasons we lust for fame.

Later, other fantasies come into play: to be loved, to be fucked, to be rich, to be immortal, to get good tables in restaurants. Fame seems at first to be a protection against the common lot of humanity. The common lot of humanity is to be a blob that rots. With fame we can outsmart decay and be embalmed for times to come.

Of course it's not really us but a version of us, an eviscerated version with all the blood and guts gone. Embalmed for posterity, like Lenin. We'll take it anyway.

And thanks. Better to be known for the wrong things than not to be known at all.

Famous people complain about fame, but they never want to give it back, myself included.

I never consciously wanted to be an actress when I was young. But when Eve Ensler and Shirley Knight approached me to be in a three-week run of *The Vagina Monologues* in New York, I said yes so quickly that I must have had hidden motives. This was my chance to get out of writing and into theater. Maybe a movie role would follow. Not that I hadn't been in one of Woody Allen's movies—but I went by so fast that nobody actually saw me. Besides, *everyone* has been in Woody's movies. There's even a web site that lists the poor slobs from other professions in Woody's movies. I believe Woody is a (sometimes misguided) genius, but that's not why we did it. Like most writers, I will do anything for a day away from the torture of the desk. As a novelist, I wanted to know viscerally what an actor's daily life is like when she is working—or so I told myself dutifully. It was bullshit. I had stardust in my addled brain. Besides, most writers are closet exhibitionists. Maybe this was a way of not having to write my next novel. When people asked me why I was impersonating a vagina for Eve, I said, "After a certain point in life, we are trapped in the métier we have chosen and there aren't many opportunities to try on other lives." Yeah, right.

So there I am, sitting on a high stool blinded by an intense spotlight. Two actors flank me on either side. We have bonded while putting on our make-up, done our good-luck rituals—a few interactive yoga postures in the wings, followed by kissing each other passionately on the lips—but now each of us is alone in her aureole of light. The lights go out on the others. I am isolated in my spotlight but for the anticipatory rustle of the audience.

My first monologue requires me to be an ancient crone who cannot call her vagina by its proper name. She can only identify it as "down there." I have found a voice for my character—God only knows where—and that voice is thoroughly Bronx, full of exploding "t"s and "p"s—a voice in which I have never before spoken. My character was prudish only in words. Her body was full of juice. Whenever a man appealed to her, she would produce a flood in her nether regions and was sure everyone could smell its odor and feel its wetness. Of course, she was the only one who could—which is the subtext of her monologue—but her juiciness so embarrassed her that she gave up men and sex forever. Comic but also tragic, this woman's story is the story of a needless, self-inflicted sacrifice. When I got the monologue right, the audience felt this. When I was too broad, the audience laughed hysterically but probably didn't understand the deeper narrative. What a responsibility an actor has. A whole life rests on her interpretation.

My next monologue required me to be a Yugoslavian girl raped in the Balkan war who feels invaded, besmirched, and wants to be spiritually cleansed. She compares her life to a river, a torrent of water. She dreams of a mountain stream cleansing her and returning her to girlhood, bringing her home. My next monologue required me to impersonate a stepmother awed by the process of witnessing her stepdaughter giving birth. For each of these I had to find the voice, the pauses, the subterranean meaning. I came to understand more about the use of voice than I ever had performing my own poems—where I was only required to be myself. And I certainly came to understand live theater in a way I never had before.

Every morning I would get up planning to write, but would find myself puttering aimlessly all day, waiting for my 5:30 p.m. pickup in the dented minibus, which was all the off-Broadway producers could afford.

The two and a half hours of preparation and make-up were essential, as was the bonding with the other actors. We talked about everything: men, politics, kids, other jobs, what we hated about our looks. We became backstage sisters. The Westside Theater has a tiny dressing area, so we were crammed together at a common dressing table, sharing space, make-up, perfume, brandy drunk straight from the bottle.

I fell in love with one of my two co-stars. Angelica Torn was a delicate pale blonde—the daughter of Geraldine Page and Rip Torn. She was pretty and intense and tortured. But it was Lauren Velez, a lush Latina with golden skin, who stirred me up. There's a sexuality backstage that makes you open yourself wide. How can you not want to fuck your fellow cast members? We three kissed each other wetly before each performance. For the first time I really understood Colette's blithe bisexuality.

The backstage world is a lot less lonely than the writer's habitual workplace. As actors, you may be terrified, but you're all in it together. After the show, there is a real sense of triumph and elation. And food tastes better than it ever does to a writer.

But the words are not yours. You don't have the anxiety of making them up from scratch, and you don't have the euphoria of putting something in the air that wasn't there before. Despite all the struggle of being a writer, the echoing void of the blank page, I also love making it up as I go along.

It's like building your own plane, then learning to fly it. Sometimes the words spill out and later make no sense at all. Sometimes they only make intermittent sense and for the next ten days you have to wrestle them into another kind of order. But sometimes their sense is utterly clear and you wonder who wrote them.

I'm glad to have moonlighted as an actor once, but I'm not planning to quit my day job. (Those offers never materialized. I'm still waiting.) Acting may be sexier, but writing is most productive when it's most mischievous. In that, writing is a lot like acting. You get ready, study, learn, memorize, rehearse and then forget all the effort and fly.

Probably all the arts are like that: intense effort, which must be absorbed into your being and never shown in the work itself. *Sprezzatura*—the art of making the difficult look easy—is the sine qua non. The actor must become the character, the painter must impersonate light and the writer must fly in a winged chariot of words. All our wings must be invisible, with no wires showing.

Like magicians, we cannot give away our tricks. When it's going well we believe we *have* no tricks and are being carried by the gods themselves.

I now realize I was moved to try live theater by Colette's example. She was the original *femme de lettres qui a mal tourné*—the woman of letters who turned out badly.

She was the one who gave up writing for theater when her first divorce forced her to earn her living on the stage. And she was the one who missed writing so much she wrote this paean to it in her book about being a reluctant performer, *The Vagabond*:

> *To write! To be able to write! It means the rapt, hypnotized gaze, caught by the reflected window of the silver inkstand. It means the burning of the divine fever on cheek and brow while a delightful death chills the hand that traces words upon the paper. It means also oblivion of time, the idle nestling in a corner of the couch while yielding free rein to a very riot of invention. It means emerging from the debauch tired and stupefied but already richly rewarded and the bearer of great wealth to be poured out upon the virgin page in the circlet of light sheltering under the lamp. . . .*
>
> *Oh, to write! That joy and torment of the idle! To write! Time and again I feel the need come upon*

me, urgent as thirst in summertime, to take notes, to depict. And I seize my pen again and begin the dangerous, deceptive game anew, seeking to capture with my flexible, double-pointed nib the sparking, fugitive, passionate words! It is merely a brief crisis, the itching of a scar.

The itching of a scar. What a perfect description of the urge to write. My little holiday in the theater also reinforced this compulsion. By leaving my métier, I also came to newly appreciate my métier. I had been sick of writing. Now I longed to return to it again. Or so I told myself.

But if you know a good agent who's looking for a woman of letters who has turned out badly, send him to me. I can always be persuaded to take some time off.

When I was in my twenties and wanted to be a writer so bad it hurt, I received a letter from a man called Louis Untermeyer who lived in Newtown, Connecticut.

"What are you doing in that mess of mediocrity?" he asked. One of my longer poems, written in Heidelberg, had appeared in some obscure poetry anthology—and Mr. Untermeyer wanted to know what else I had written.

I recognized his name from poetry anthologies and textbooks from my high school and college days. His anthologies of American and British poetry were so ubiquitous that even the Russian poet Joseph Brodsky had one of them with him in exile in a labor camp north of the Arctic Circle. Brodsky studied it with the help of a dictionary. And learned about English poetry that way. Louis Untermeyer was famous—though I didn't yet know the full extent of his fame. Nor did I know that he was my grandfather's age. After some letters back and forth and some poems I proffered, Louis Untermeyer pronounced me the real thing and invited me to his house in Connecticut for lunch.

I boned up on him. He was a prodigious anthologist and translator, the author of many books of poetry early in his career, the former editor of the Marxist journal *The Masses,* a witty guest on *What's My Line?* (fired in the fifties for his leftist affiliations) and a supporter of Robert Frost, Carl Sandburg, Ezra Pound and many others. He adored poetry, wisecracks, conversation—as I was to learn when I took him up on his offer and visited him in Newtown.

I found an energetic nonagenarian, a twinkling old gent with an eye for young blondes, living with his fifth wife, Bryna. We talked of poetry while Bryna brought us a delicious lunch and joined intermittently in the conversation.

From then on, Louis became my poetry adviser and mail-order critic. Allan Jong, my second husband, and I were frequent visitors to the Untermeyers' Connecticut house. It was there that we met Arthur Miller and Inge Morath, Bette and Howard Fast, Muriel Rukeyser, the choreographer Martha Clarke, the director Arvin Brown and his actress wife, Joyce Ebert, as well as the actress Teresa Wright and her playwright husband, Robert Anderson. Dozens of other writers, actors and directors were guests at the Untermeyers. Because of Louis, I became friends with Howard and Bette Fast, who were to introduce me to their son, Jon, who became my third husband and the father of my daughter Molly.

Because of Louis I became friends with Arthur Miller and Inge Morath. "I guess we love each other because Louis loved us both," Arthur said to me at a memorial service for Louis. I thought of that typically ironic, self-deprecating Arthur Millerism when I went to a memorial for Arthur at the Majestic Theater in New York.

Memorial services are funny things. Some are there for love and some for careerism. At Arthur's, most seemed to be there for love. Oh, there were plenty of stars—Mike Nichols, Kurt Vonnegut, John Guare, Tony Kushner, Edward Albee, Daniel Day-Lewis . . . but since Arthur was the presiding spirit, there was love in the air.

I remembered that Inge had once told me that when Arthur first asked her out, she was reluctant to go because he seemed to be in so much trouble. She believed in the maxim *Never fuck anyone with more troubles than yourself.* He was living at the Chelsea Hotel, post Marilyn Monroe, and was so depressed that Inge worried. She dated him against her better judgment and fell in love with "the integrity of his mind." It was easy to fall in love with. He was what he seemed. His writing and his self were not divided. Arthur's integrity was everywhere represented in his memorial service—and his friendships. Fame had not turned him into an asshole.

Some great writers are bastards. Some are towers of narcissism. Arthur had a gift for friendship that was born out of his fierce modesty. He was a carpenter as well as a playwright, and the two informed each other. Rebecca Miller read a poem of her father's that was both about playwrighting and about carpentry. Arthur speaks of the wood he is fashioning into a useful object: "I endure even as I disappear" is the last line.

Tony Kushner pointed out that Arthur believed "when you speak, God is listening." Edward Albee remembered that Arthur thought writing was only worth pursuing if it had "relevance to human survival."

Memorial services are important for the living rather than the dead because they make us ask ourselves, *Have we done everything we're supposed to do?* Time is running out. We're next.

"I am sick and tired of old men dreaming up wars for young men to die in," George McGovern remembered Arthur saying. He said it while Vietnam raged, but it's even more relevant now. "Attention must be paid," as Arthur wrote in *Death of a Salesman*. For writers as well as other people, "integrity of mind" is the most important attribute.

We live in a time when the most exalted lie most blatantly and nobody seems to care. Integrity has become an old-fashioned word. Integrity of mind is not even sought by most writers. As William Sloane Coffin said of Arthur Miller, "his absence is everywhere present."

Poet Honor Moore quoted Arthur as saying, "When life disappointed me, I always had my writing." Writing was not a choice but a need.

One summer in Venice, two decades ago, I ran into Anthony Burgess, sitting at a café on the *fondamenta* in Giudecca and spinning tales for a British camera crew. He was filming a documentary for U.K. television. I stayed to listen. I knew Burgess through our mutual French translators, Georges Belmont and Hortense Chabrier, and he had been a fervent champion of my work—particularly my eighteenth-century fantasy, *Fanny*. Burgess was always worth listening to. His erudition was astounding. So was his wit.

After the filming, I invited Burgess and his wife, Liana, to a party my friend Liselotte Höhs, the artist, was giving for me. Anthony came, received the praise of his Italian and American readers, but stayed only an hour.

"I have to write," he said, and he disappeared back to his place on the Giudecca. Liana stayed.

Anthony was forever running back to his room to write prose or compose his daily music. He was incapable of not writing. Then he developed cancer and died.

Last summer, after I spoke about him at the first Anthony Burgess Symposium in Manchester, England (his birthplace), his widow Liana warned my husband: "Don't let her write so much. Writing shortened my husband's life."

"I couldn't stop her from writing even if I wanted to," Ken said. "Besides, it makes her happy."

"Life is more important than writing," Liana said.

"I hope not to have to choose," I said.

No one in America is immune to show business. Maybe no one in the world is. We all hope our boring lives will be transformed by the thrill of performing for other people. And fame, riches and everlasting love will follow. For me there has been some truth in that. But not in the way I first thought.

Even babies respond to the camera with gleeful exhibitionism. My grandson Max shines when the camera comes his way, so did Molly. So do my nieces and nephews. The camera creates a magical transformation. It's not enough to exist; we must chronicle that existence. From the Lascaux cave painters to the latest plump-lipped, skinny-hipped starlet—the need to duplicate our loves and fears is irresistible. Narrative- and image-making creatures like humans don't feel any experience is complete unless it's recorded.

Dolphins, whales and chimps don't seem to have this need—though their intelligence may be higher than ours. I certainly hope so. We have shown ourselves to be a delusional, self-destructive species.

When my first novel developed a buzz—in galleys—

all sorts of new people burst into my life. The wonderful composer of *Gypsy*, *Gentlemen Prefer Blondes*, *Funny Girl* and hundreds of songs I loved, like "Three Coins in the Fountain," "Let It Snow, Let It Snow, Let It Snow," "I Fall in Love Too Easily" and "The Things We Did Last Summer," Jule Styne was by then a pretty old guy—but he entertained me at Sardi's with his dreams of a musical based on *Fear of Flying*. "Isadora dances onto the stage where seven couches are lined up in seven colors. She lies down on each couch in turn and sings her troubles to seven psychoanalysts, who get up and dance with her before she dances offstage."

He mimed it for me in the aisles around our up-front table, while all the Sardi's gawkers gawked. Jule was cute and short and lecherous and I was mad not to take him up on it. It would have made my father so happy. It would have made me so happy to work with such a huge talent. But my agent discouraged me, saying there was no up-front money in musicals, and I was dumb enough to listen. Who cared about up-front money? Certainly not I. I have always disdained cash in favor of credit. Perhaps I even feel guilty when I make too much money. Money has never principally motivated me. I knew that my father gave up music for money and always regretted it. I was determined not to do the same. Besides, the movie deal my agents had in store wouldn't finally make me much money anyway, as it turned out.

I was romanced also by the producer of *The Godfather* and by the producer of *Judgement at Nuremberg*—but I was blind and deaf. At that point (1973), I was mostly confused. Some reviews were great and some were so vitriolic they made me wince. I had left the academic world and found a jungle so red in tooth and claw that I was astounded. Not that the academic world is kind. No world is kind. But I was buffeted between praise and blame, and in those days I had no idea how to cope.

Jule Styne may have seemed elderly to me, but he had another twenty years of big hits in him. Instead, I listened to the people at ICM, who wanted me to meet a certain Julia Phillips who had just won an Oscar for producing *The Sting*.

Julia flew in from "the Coast" to meet me. (She probably had other fish to fry, but this was how my agents presented it.) Enter Julia, a short, spiky-haired bundle of energy who could not sit still, and smoked, as my grandmother used to say, "like a chimney." Julia was tough, smart, obsessed with herself, saw the whole world as a battlefield and had a serious drug problem. But that was long before I understood anything about drug problems.

When she crossed her legs and sat in a chair, she couldn't stop shaking her crossed leg. When she started talking, she couldn't stop. When she started working, she couldn't sleep. Had I known anything at all, I would have recognized the signs of cocaine addiction.

She was pretty, with a squarish face, brownish hair and bright green eyes. She talked tough. She bowled me over with her moxie. She seemed to have no doubts in the world about herself or anything. Who could tell it was the cocaine talking?

Hollywood was rife with cocaine in those days. Nobody saw the big picture—the ruined lives, the car crashes, the bloody noses, the fried brains.

So Julia and I started working in her suite at the Sherry-Netherland. We took my novel and broke it down into scenes on index cards. We laid those index cards out on the floor and tried to decide what was essential and what should go. As we worked, Julia fielded endless calls—from her husband, from her studio head (a certain David Begelman, who later shot himself in a hotel room), from her lawyer (a certain Norman Geary, who also later shot himself), from her mother, from her father, from her daughter's nanny. Julia was one of those people for whom phone calls are public statements to those who are compelled to listen. Since the advent of the cell phone, there are many more such people. But I had never before met one.

I listened in awe as Julia was ferocious to her studio head, her lawyer, her nanny, her mother, her husband. I was horrified, but my demon was impressed. My demon had always whispered to me that I would be thinner and richer if I took less shit from people. Here was a woman who took shit from no one.

This was 1973 and times were a-changin'. Like Billie Jean King, competitive women wanted to take on their male counterparts and win. Julia seemed to embody that change. She was a woman who called the shots. And she was smart—in a brassy sort of way. No graduate school for her. She had jumped feetfirst into the world of work— publishing, then movies. As my agents said, she was a "comer"—mentioning only later that they also represented her.

As we worked, Julia fantasized about the directors who would be perfect for this script—Stanley Donen, who did the brilliant *Two for the Road*; John Schlesinger of *Darling*, *Midnight Cowboy* and *Sunday, Bloody Sunday* fame; Hal Ashby, who'd recently directed *Harold and Maude*. Other names were bandied about, like Warren Beatty's and Steven Spielberg's. Julia appeared to know them and what they were currently doing. She was on a first-name basis with all of them. I was dazzled, as I was meant to be. After dealing with my book, her next "project" was to be something about UFOs with Spielberg.

"Do you know the phrase 'Close Encounters of the Third Kind'?" she asked.

I didn't. Nobody did yet.

Julia thought that *Fear of Flying* was the story of her life. I was beginning to hear that from a lot of people—including my prescient paperback publisher, Elaine Koster, who saved my book from obscurity by demanding a sizable first printing and ads and more galleys (those early uncorrected proofs circulated in the publishing industry). Suddenly there were women in the business who had the power to make books happen. There had been none of them a few years before. But a few years before, *Fear of Flying* might not have been published. Suddenly, everyone was interested in women—what we thought, what we felt, what we wanted. I remembered my college days when Anatole Broyard told us we couldn't be writers, so I knew this sudden rush could just as easily evaporate. If women were madly in style, I knew we could be madly out of style. I took all this enthusiasm with many grains of salt. Besides, I had grown up in a family of depressives who joked to keep from killing themselves.

After the two weeks at the Sherry with Julia, I went home to start to write the screenplay while she went back to her daughter and husband in Malibu. We talked endlessly on the phone. I struggled with my first-ever script while the deal dragged on and on—with more agents and lawyers piling on all the time. Drafts of legal papers went back and forth. There were no faxes then, so bulging envelopes, sent "by hand," were always heaped on my doorstep. Legal bills went up and up, but still there was no contract, no check. I had no idea this was the way of most movie deals.

Contract or no contract, I believed that having worked with Julia made me committed to her. It never occurred to me I could walk if I didn't like the deal.

Plenty of other stuff was on my mind. My marriage to Allan Jong was in its death throes. Not that it ever had been good. My main reason for marrying him was that he was a shrink and my first husband had been schizophrenic. We had practically nothing in common and he had been involved with another woman almost as long as we were together.

My novel kept hitting the lower reaches of the bestseller list—consisting of only ten places then—and going out of stock. I didn't know it at the time, but my publisher, Aaron Asher, was in the process of leaving the company and no one had the authority to reprint my damn book. It had struck a nerve—but no one could find it. (By then, John Updike had praised it in *The New Yorker,* writing the kind of review most first novelists can only dream of.) I was dazed.

Answered prayers are, above all, bewildering. Looking back, I remember that I was more panicked than elated. I was sure I'd be hit by a bus or mugged in Central Park. That's what early notoriety feels like—at least at first. Only much, much later do you discover some pleasures in being recognized—the good tables in restaurants, the people who swear you changed their lives—and by then your fame has faded.

And then there were fans. I never really expected to become famous for my first novel—much as I fantasized about it. I was a young poet, and poetry then as now is a recipe for obscurity. Certainly I could never have imagined the strange sort of fame the fates had in store for me. I was absolutely inundated with cries for help, sexual propositions and vicious attacks. For some people, I became representative of all that was wrong with the world and young women. For others, I was the prophet of their rebirth. It was at once disconcerting and ecstatic. I spent at least a year answering reams of correspondence from the frustrated and lovelorn before I realized that my most heartfelt replies only provoked more relentless demands. I was in danger of becoming a sort of Ms. Lonelyhearts; I had to stop.

At a distance of more than three decades, I now see demands of fame *cannot* be met. What you evoke in a fan is by its nature unfulfillable. You tap into a certain hunger, a certain yearning. It is fierce and powerful, but it has almost nothing to do with you. The more you attempt to appease it, the more furious the fan becomes. It's the reason relations between fans and their obsessional objects can turn so dark and murderous. I had to throw the boxes of mail away before I could even think of writing again.

Around that time, I was sent by my publisher to meet the talent booker for Johnny Carson's *Tonight Show*. I waited in a cubicle while the great booker finished a phone call. Then I was ushered in.

"So," she snapped, "why should you be on the *Tonight Show*? What's the book about?"

"It's about a young woman who wants to be a writer and how she overcomes her fears and learns to be independent. It's about husbands and wives, wives and lovers, and . . ."

"That's enough," the booker said. "Johnny isn't interested in human relationships."

The follow-up to that rejection story occurred just this past year when my publisher took me to lunch with the premier talent booker on another national show.

I arrived first, clutching a very obscure and annoying German book whose author had just won the Nobel Prize. I tried to read it while waiting for my publisher. But I was too jumpy. Why are Nobel Prize authors so infuriating? Either they are grim to the point of making you want to kill yourself (Coetzee) or so obscure that even the English translations seem written in another language.

Should I have arrived late to make an entrance? I am really nervous. My publisher finally arrives—just in time to see the chef appear to tell me I am his favorite writer and bring a complimentary tranche of foie gras for my delectation. I thank him profusely and promise to send him autographed books. I pick at the foie gras, checking my watch. My publisher and I are both frazzled.

"Are we being stood up?" I ask him.

"Don't jump to conclusions," he says. But he seems nervous too.

We order wine in the daytime because we are both so rattled. We try to talk, but we are looking at the entrance to see if we are being stood up. The minutes pass. It's not possible that the talent booker chose a restaurant in his own office building only to arrive late. That would be a real slap in the face. Get my publisher to come from SoHo and me from the Upper East Side just to prove his power. Or perhaps he isn't coming at all? Perhaps he forgot the appointment? My publisher and I make stilted conversation. Normally easy with each other, we are poisoned by the talent booker's lateness. After a nerve-wracking, shifty-eyed, twenty-minute wait together, I ask him to go downstairs to look for our guest. Never meet a talent booker in a restaurant with Dantean levels! Not there, he says. I hand him my cell phone. (Why doesn't he have his own?) He calls the booker's office, calls every number he can think of. Is this my publisher's fault? Has he fucked up or have I become obscure? Are other tables listening? Are they aware this is Judgment Day for us? Eventually the maître d', with that instinctual maître d' intuition, comes over to make nice and compliment my jewelry. The chef appears again with another brilliant complimentary dish—snails in champagne this time. I tell my publisher to keep calling and he does—calls office after office only to find everyone out to lunch.

Thirty-five minutes late, the talent booker arrives

with barely an excuse—"in a meeting I couldn't get out of"—and starts telling us a long, involved story about how he was underpaid and finally got a substantial raise because a superstar at his network intervened for him. The implication is that we couldn't do anything for him. We are chopped liver. We need him much more than he needs us and our thirty-five minutes of waiting rubs our noses in this messy truth. He asks my publisher snottily if he does anything besides "coffee-table books," as if he were a nobody from a nowhere publishing house. We both feel chastened, though in fact we've done nothing wrong except pursue rather than be pursued. We showed abject weakness. Always let them pursue you even if it means losing some media buzz.

This is fame in New York. Every encounter is a calibration of your current worth. Nothing is neutral. If you were insecure before you got famous, you'll be twice as insecure now. No one has ever bettered Hemingway's description of literary New York: *a jar of tapeworms feeding on each other.*

"So how *are* you?" the talent booker asks, knowing the answer.

"I'm fine," I lie.

. . .

ERICA JONG

When I started to publish in the seventies, serious authors disdained TV. TV was considered low-class and tacky. Now TV is even lower class and tackier, but authors—including me—will go on any program that will have them just to get exposure—if they are lucky enough to be invited. This is because books have gone so far down the food chain that any TV show is better than bringing out a book with no exposure at all.

My first TV experience came in 1973 with *Fear of Flying*. I was flown to Detroit—which at that point was the asshole of America. The taxi driver taking me to the TV station told me that my host (whose name I forget) was famous for "talkin' to women about their organzi."

"Organzi?"

"Yeah—he's the first person to say 'organzi' on TV. Very controversial."

"Oh, I see. 'Orgasm.'"

"Yeah, organzi."

The TV studio is icy cold. Mr. Organzi is taping five shows that day and I am the last in line, so I wait and wait. Finally, I am taken into the frigid studio, where I confront a grizzled, gray newsman who has modeled his broadcasting style on Walter Winchell's.

"Come meet Erica Younnnng. Who has caused quite a stir with her brash, abrasive and potty-mouthed novel." ("Potty-mouthed" is a term I abhor, smacking as it does of toilet training as a metaphor for speech.)

> MR. ORGANZI: *Admit it, you're a lesbian. You hate men.*
>
> JONG: *I don't hate men at all.*
>
> ORGANZI: *But in your book you say that men and women will never work. To me that means you are a lesbian.*

At this point, I would have walked out, but walking out of a taped show doesn't do the trick. But I was so beaten down and scared that I began muttering like a graduate student about Joyce and Proust, as I do when I am terrified.

Once Merv Griffin invited me on his television show only to ask me if I really wanted to pee standing up.

"Isn't that what all you women's libbers want?"

He had surrounded me with old Hollywood dames like Adela Rogers St. Johns who claimed that they had never suffered discrimination as women. That was what some TV shows did in the early seventies—brought out old warhorses to prove that feminism was a lie.

Now that we live in the age of reality TV, inevitably someone will create a reality TV show about writers. The problem will be how uneventful and unvisual a writer's life is. In movies, the writer sits at a typewriter, typing a few words and then noisily seizing the paper out of the roller, balling it up and throwing it on the floor. This is the way Jane Fonda played Lillian Hellman in *Pentimento*. But now that we use computers instead of typewriters, we don't even have the noise of the roller to add to the drama.

In the reality TV show *Writer!*, producers will be hard pressed to find a resident hunk or ingenue, because writers are usually not so good to look at. Manic and self-conscious, the writers inevitably will spend part of the show locked in the bathroom, unwilling to face the cameras. The camera pans to the unattended computer, as in an endless Andy Warhol epic. But eventually one writer will rise to the challenge and reveal the writer's true life: She looks at her Amazon rating and despairs. She flips through books for inspiration. She polishes all the shoes in the house. She masturbates. She squeezes her blackheads even if she doesn't have any blackheads. Then she puts a gun in her mouth and commits suicide in gonzo fashion like Hunter Thompson. For one night, the ratings go through the roof. Then they plummet again, because you can't have a writer committing suicide every week—and what else can a writer do that is visually captivating?

No sooner had I written this fantasy than I opened the newspaper to see writers competing to be locked up in Long Island City for thirty days in something called "the Flux Factory" so that they could turn out novels in that period. Spectators are allowed to watch. "We're exploring what it is to be a writer," says Morgan Meis, who is the "curator" of the exhibit, which is called, imaginatively, "Novel." Here I thought I was kidding and someone's actually doing it! But of course to show an exhibit of a novel-in-progress, you'd have to be inside the novelist's brain—a far more exotic place than the Flux Factory. The whole point of imaginative writing is that it is neither time-bound nor place-bound. Novelists writing are not that different from lawyers or students writing.

And the process of writing, duh, takes place in the mind. Our outer lives are not that different from the outer lives of other people. It's our inner lives that matter.

Despite the boringness of our lives, writers do have fans, but we may wonder what these fans are really seeking.

Once I got a letter from a fan saying that since his wife died he had been very lonely so could I please send him my soiled underwear for him to sniff? He had gotten the idea because his wife's underwear was very comforting to him, but now that he had worn it out with sniffing would I kindly send mine? Another letter from the president "at very large" of a club called The Hung Jury invited me to be the "Mistress of Measurements." It was clear from my books, he wrote, that I was a "size queen" and he was sure I'd enjoy these measurements very much. I have also been followed by stalkers, deluged with photographs of naked men and solicited by the dodgiest of charities. After a while, I stopped answering fan mail entirely.

Now, I loved authors who gave me pleasure and I kissed their pictures, but it never would have occurred to me to reach out for their underwear or their personal attendance upon my genitals. In fact, I had rarely written to an author before I became one. They seemed to inhabit another world. What was it about my work that inspired such requests?

I want to be loved, and sometimes being loved seems to imply breaking down the barrier between author and reader. But something else was happening here. What these requests seemed to imply was a literal-mindedness all my work decried. I am sure there are plenty of readers who love my work and would never think of making such requests—for which I am grateful. But the crazier readers do reveal something about the link between reader and writer: the desire to pass through the covers of a book into someone else's imaginary world. These odd requests are really saying "Rescue me." If only I could.

The idea of escaping into a book and running away with the author or the characters is something we've all felt. We find the fantasy in *Peter Pan,* in *Mary Poppins,* in *The Wizard of Oz,* in fairy tales like "The Twelve Dancing Princesses." What if we could enter that magical world, come back, and the only sign of our trespass into the magic was worn shoe leather or a scarf carelessly left in the scene on the mantelpiece plate? We all want to move between dream and reality with such ease.

I certainly do. If I could go to sleep one night, wake up in Renaissance Venice and have an affair with William Shakespeare . . . well, at least I could write a book about it. Is the desire to write very close to the desire to escape? Is that why the compulsion is so strong? The world we live in is appalling. Can there be a better one somewhere?

Probably this is also what fans want. The link between the writer and the fan is one of shared fantasy. The writer seems to paint a world where the fan's problems vanish. The writer is doing this for herself, but the fan thinks it is especially for him, and that's where trouble and disappointment enter the picture. If you are sane, you know the world of the book is invented. It is not a tangible place but an escape into fantasy.

That's why being a writer has meant forays into the realm of demons. That's why it's such a dangerous profession. In order to make the world of fantasy real, you have to believe in it yourself—at least for the time you're writing the book.

So, Julia Phillips and I met in California several months after our work at the Sherry. By then it was late autumn and my book had caught fire in paperback and was everywhere, selling something like three million copies in the first three months. I had the rough script of the novel with me. She was too jumpy to read it. She picked me up at the airport, deposited me at the Beverly Hills Hotel, made an appointment with me for the next day, then took off for points unknown. She was always taking off for points unknown in those days.

I looked around my room dazed from jet lag, made some phone calls—one to the Fasts, who were organizing a party for me the next night; one to Henry Miller, whom I was to meet the day after; one to my husband, Allan Jong, in New York, who was going to sleep. I wandered out into the lobby and then to the street, hoping to walk a bit. But there was no place to walk. I went to the pool to see who was there. Any stars? No one. Only the moon rising and the soft air of Beverly Hills, promising magic. Imagine how New Yorkers who came to this place in the teens and twenties must have felt—when the air was full of orange blossoms or the smell of smudge pots, the whole town an orchard on the edge of the desert.

I never arrive in California without thinking of that era—of Charlie Chaplin and Douglas Fairbanks and Mary Pickford—and the freedom the West Coast seemed to offer. Now Los Angeles is a sprawling city of impossible traffic, but even in the seventies you could sense what it once had been to the old movie colony coming West. It was a place to reinvent yourself in the desert air. It was the West—land of sunset and dreams. Never mind that the West had represented death to the ancient Egyptians and ancient Greeks.

I went to sleep thinking of that era, intoxicated by

California as everyone is, at first. The last time I'd been in California was to transport my first husband to the loony bin. I had my father and a shrink in tow. And the time before that, I was with my parents, staying at the Bel-Air on the way to a summer in Japan before I started Barnard. It seems to me now that I was always in California at important crossroads in my life. New York was home. The Coast, like Venice, was an incarnation of *away*. It's always easier to change your life while *away*.

The next day, Julia was to meet me for lunch at the Polo Lounge, but she never showed. She called several times, saying she was late for several different reasons. She didn't make it to lunch, to tea, to drinks—always with a new excuse. I tried to work on the script but didn't know where to begin. It was not a bad script, but, like all scripts, it needed work. I tried to reach Julia. Her assistant was evasive and the housekeeper at her beach house spoke no English.

I whiled the day away somehow. Then, at five-thirty or so, Howard Fast called to say he was sending his son, Jonathan, to pick me up.

I often know in an instant the people who are going to change my life.

Jonathan Fast drove under the portico of the Beverly Hills Hotel in a green MG, smiled at me with his toothy smile, and I knew I was going to marry him, have a child with him and live happily ever after. Well—so that part was wrong.

As we drove up through the canyon to his parents' house on Laurel Way, I stared at his profile and tried to figure out *how* I knew my life was never going to be the same.

We went to the party—a huge gang bang full of radiant movie stars, pale, hunched-over writers and Zen Buddhist disciples of Howard's.

Howard meditated daily, to little effect. If he sought detachment, he never found it. A more *attached* individual never lived on this fickle planet. He worshiped Zen masters because he was their polar opposite, a man who wanted to shackle everything to himself—his children, his wife, his grandchildren. There never was such a contradictory spirit, a proponent of freedom who practiced slavery on his family, a communist turned capitalist, a practitioner of open marriage who couldn't let his wife out of his sight. Some of his books are wonderful: *Spartacus, Being Red, The Hessian, The Jews*. I hardly pretend to have read all seventy-five of them. He was an extraordinary historical novelist. I understood Roman crucifixion better after reading *Spartacus* than after reading any book about Jesus, including the New Testament.

And Howard was *brave*. Standing up to the House Un-American Activities Committee was valiant in a way we can hardly imagine now. We forget that there were many who believed more in their swimming pools and Rolls-Royces than in free speech—and Howard was definitely not among them. He went to jail. He moved to Mexico when he was blacklisted. He endured the bitterness of his longtime publisher telling him regarding *Spartacus*, "I dare not even open the manuscript because I know it's brilliant and there's no way I can publish it and risk having us closed down." Howard had the guts to publish it himself under the Blue Heron imprint. And when it became a famous book, Howard always said that Kirk Douglas paid as little as possible for the movie rights.

Bette, Howard's wife, had more than a gift for entertaining, for cooking, for warmth, for making people mingle. She continued to be a working artist when there was no room for two artists in that household. If she did indeed have a torrid affair with Dashiell Hammett, God bless her. I only hope she did—but perhaps Dash was too drunk. (Jon and I found a copy of *The Maltese Falcon* tenderly inscribed to her.) Howard certainly provoked her with his many movie-star adulteries. All this is hindsight. At the time, I thought of Howard as a leftist saint.

Jonathan and I lost each other, then kept trying to

find each other in the crowd of actors, producers and writers. I talked to Irving Wallace and his wife, Sylvia, to Howard's latest blond squeeze, always looking over my shoulder to see where Jonathan was. After two hours or so, we escaped the party and drove to the top of Mulholland to watch the lights of Los Angeles twinkling in the smog.

We spoke about marriage, whether a true marriage of minds and bodies was possible. It astonishes me to remember this—how quickly we got into the subject of our being together. It was as if we both knew the future— and the future was Molly. Someday, scientists will understand how this works—pheromones?—how a man and woman meet and know instantly that they will have a child together. Anyway, we fell in love ferociously and violently—and went back to the pink adobe palace to plight our troth.

The marriage didn't last, but we loved each other for a long time, hated each other for a long time and finally made peace when three of our four parents died and our grandson was born. I cannot say that we are best friends, but we are happy to talk and joke and e-mail, to spend holidays together with Molly and her family and to mutually adore Max.

I remember Jon's ferocious sense of humor when I

hear Molly's acid jokes. And I love him for fathering this amazing woman. Without him I might not have had the courage. The best part of getting older is this: watching the circles get completed and former enemies or lovers join hands again.

Julia didn't call the next day or the next. I tried to reach her but struck out. Finally, I took my studio-rented car and drove to Pacific Palisades to meet Henry Miller, my pen pal.

Henry had started writing to me a year before. In his first missive, he announced that I had written the female version of *Tropic of Cancer*—so of course I had to read it. When I did, I found it nothing whatever like my novel. *Tropic of Cancer*—like all Henry's books—was a wild mélange of free association, word cadenzas and philo-sophical rants, spoken by an antihero who is always looking for the secret of life in the unlikeliest places. Its reputation as dirty book astonished me. It was no dirtier than *Portnoy's Complaint* or *Couples*. By 1974, literary sex was ubiquitous. Of course, this was partly the doing of Henry Miller, whose books were repatriated to his home country in 1962, thanks to Barney Rosset, his pub-lisher at Grove Press, and other literary pioneers.

What troubled people, I thought, was Miller's ability to break his head open and show the maggots within. Also, Henry Miller declared himself "the happiest man alive"—and it's verboten for writers to be happy. We are supposed to be miserable. How dare the happiest man alive presume to be a writer? Didn't he know the rules? Apparently not. He neither knew nor cared. This insouciance was the ultimate transgression. He was oblivious of the etiquette of literary life. He didn't care about genre. He thought fiction and autobiography were one and the same. He predicted, in fact, that in the future the lines between genres would disappear—as they have—and he refused to recognize distinctions he thought were stupid. He was hated not so much for his sexual transgressions as for his exuberance. Well, maybe there was a resemblance there after all.

I've always thought that the idea of genre was a blot on the soul of literature. Categories like novel, memoir, biography have no value when you're writing—however much value they may have to librarians or bookstores. A book is a book is a book. I suspect that the idea of genres has silenced more writers than it has liberated. Even the *idea* of a book is daunting, which may be why Jack Kerouac wrote on those endless rolls. Think of the idea of a book and you will immediately think of what's permitted and what is not permitted. What you want is to write what has not been written before, or why bother? "There is only one thing which interests me vitally now, and that is the recording of all that which is omitted in books," Henry Miller said in *Tropic of Cancer.* And then he proceeded to do so:

> *This then? This is not a book. This is libel, slander, defamation of character. This is not a book in the ordinary sense of the word. No, this is . . . a gob of spit in the face of Art, a kick in the pants to God, Man, Destiny, Time, Love, Beauty.*

I suspect that an author must always feel this way to create anything original.

The novel when new in the eighteenth century was thought to be a low and tawdry form, suitable only for serving maids. Henry Fielding wrote his novels as mock epics in the hopes of elevating them to literature. He convinced himself that his epic trappings would fool his readers into thinking his novels were art. But with Fielding, as with later novelists, it is the story, not the trappings, that matters.

People have been telling each other stories since cave days. Wondering what to call these stories is the least of our problems. We only want them to be entertaining. And illuminating.

I've never begun a book without having grave doubts about the form in which I was writing. I thought of *Fear of Flying* as a rant rather than a novel. I always hoped to find a way to tell a story partly in poetry and partly in prose. The closest I came was *Sappho's Leap*, in which Sappho's fragments are used as road markers in the plot. I always admired Nabokov for having found a way to tell an entire story in footnotes in his wonderful *Pale Fire*. The urge to reinvent forms is endemic in writers. The novel is endlessly elastic. It can take all sorts of playfulness and switches in perspective and still be a novel. In the last few decades it has merged into the memoir (or the memoir has flowed into it). Poems can be part of a novel. All kinds of digressions can be accommodated as long as they illustrate character and don't stop the music. All that matters is that the voice be consistent (or intelligently inconsistent) and that the reader wants to turn the page. The reader turning the page is the only sine qua non.

So I drove to Pacific Palisades, parked my car on a shady street and knocked on the door of 444 Ocampo

Drive, refusing to obey the admonishment on the front door that encouraged passersby to move on rather than bother the ancient sage within.

Henry didn't mean it. He loved guests. They kept him alive. I knocked and knocked. When no one answered, I opened the door hesitantly and let myself in.

Twinka Thiebaud heard me. A beautiful redhead in her twenties, the daughter of Wayne Thiebaud, the artist, she knew immediately who I was, embraced me and told me how much she loved *Fear of Flying*. She ushered me into a room with a Ping-Pong table and Henry's watercolors all over the walls and ran to get Henry.

Several minutes later, he appeared. An old man in a bathrobe and slippers, pushed in a wheelchair by a gorgeous young woman, he immediately began to talk and didn't stop until exhaustion set in and he had to go back to sleep. He rattled on about Brooklyn, the Village, Paris, Greece—a torrent of words, words, words that turned into rivers, lava flows, mountains, valleys. He took me from his father's tailor shop in Brooklyn to the Cosmodemonic Telegraph Company, from Anaïs Nin's house in Louviciennes to Clichy to the Villa Seurat to Greek islands cleansed by sunlight. He talked until he could talk no more. Then he loaded me down with gifts—watercolors, books, posters—which he inscribed to me: "To Erica bursting with talent." Then Twinka took him back to his bedroom in his wheelchair.

Later he would tell me that, in those years, his head was full of the most erotic fantasies, which he could no longer act on. But I knew how alive he was. My most lasting impression was that I had met one of the most exuberant souls who ever landed on Earth.

I think it's almost impossible for a young person to get into the head of an old person. If we could, the world would never go forward, nor would it change. The old are perhaps younger in mind than we. But their bodies have rebelled against them, and while we still have our eyes, our legs, our ears, we cannot imagine this. We think our material selves will last forever. The old know better. They know that nothing lasts but words, music and color. The rest is just a pile of bones and teeth and a dark spot on the ground.

So two days in Los Angeles and I had met my mentor and the father of my daughter. But not my producer. I had no idea what had become of her.

And so it went. I joined the Fast and Miller families. I did television shows for my book—by now a runaway best-seller in paperback—and I agonized about leaving

Allan Jong, which I had known for years I was someday going to do. How could I not do it now? I had been reborn as a Henry Miller protégée.

It's strange to me that certain times in our lives present a multitude of impossible choices all at once. Only in retrospect do we know that it was all part of some plan. We think we are undecided, but the anxiety of indecision is a smoke screen the gods put before our eyes so we won't be paralyzed by fear.

Change is terrifying—and necessary. How do we accomplish it despite the terror?

I wish I could say that Henry had the answer, because he writes a lot about life-changing risks taken and survived. But it is really Homer who has the answer. The gods put mists of their own making before our eyes so that we can do what we are meant to do without fear stopping us. The mists can be made of sex, of filial love, of witchcraft. Without them, we would never leave home. Or return.

Julia came back. We had a lunch in which she apologized profusely and then we drove out to Malibu to meet her adorable baby, Kate. We had dinner with the Dunnes, Joan Didion and John Gregory Dunne, who were lovely, but we never did get to work on the screenplay, despite Julia's promises.

"I have notes for you," she kept saying. But somehow she could never find them. Things kept coming up—dinners, parties, babysitting crises. Still, I thought we'd get to work eventually. And before long, it was time to fly back to New York together.

"We'll take the red-eye."

"The what?"

"The last plane that gets you to New York at dawn." I was learning a whole new vocabulary with her. "Red-eye," "projects," "pay or play," "A-list, B-list," "green light."

"Just wait till *Fear of Flying* gets the green light," she said. "Then we'll really have fun."

"How does that happen?"

"An A-list director attached. And a star. It will all come together at the party tomorrow night. Don't wear your usual *schmatte*. This party is totally A-list."

"You never told me about the party."

"I forgot. But Streisand is coming and Goldie Hawn. They both want to play Isadora."

I panicked. I had nothing to wear.

Somehow, I got packed (we were leaving for LAX right from the party), laid out what I thought was my chicest dress and said my good-byes to Jon Fast and his parents, Twinka Thiebaud, and Henry Miller and his kids.

My clothes were all wrong. The women would be wearing skin-tight jeans, skimpy silk tops and Elsa Peretti Diamonds by the Yard. They would be carrying Hermès bags, towering over me in platform shoes. The New York shabby-poet style I affected in those days (to hide my success from the grad students and literati who were my friends) might be O.K. for the 92nd Street Y and poetry seminars with Mark Strand and Stanley Kunitz at Columbia. But it was dowdy by Hollywood standards. And I was way too *fat* for Hollywood. I vowed to go on a strict diet immediately. The Coast was unforgiving of women's looks. Facials and expensive haircuts were de rigueur. We were not yet up to face-lifts—most of us. Nor breast implants, nor chin implants, nor skin resurfacing. But the clothes and the grooming were all expensive.

Every métier has its rules of attraction. Young Hollywood in the seventies was no different. Only certain handbags would do (Hermès, Gucci). And the pearls my mother had bought me in Japan were too conservative. Besides, I had neither my personal hairdresser, my personal facialist nor my personal drug dealer.

Parties scare me anyway. But parties with A-list stars? I knew how to chat up people in my own milieu, but what on earth would I say on Mount Olympus?

Naturally, I got too drunk and stoned—as I used to do in those days—and afterward I couldn't remember what I said to anyone. Not Goldie Hawn, not Barbra Streisand, not Warren Beatty. In fact, I was afraid to even greet Beatty because his sexual reputation preceded him. And Steven Spielberg, incredibly, was not yet legendary— just a promising young director. And my childhood friend Nessa Hyams was there—the first woman executive at Columbia. So I should have felt comfortable. But I was not.

Julia kept coming by saying, "Look who I brought for you. Look who came out for you." It was her achievement to get all these people together in one room. It was a testament to her power. People met at parties are hardly people met. Everyone is acting. Everyone is on. Everyone is there for reasons other than friendship. But I still have no idea why I was so naive and gullible. I think it was because of my father and what I thought he wanted me to be.

Now I know that famous people are as hungry for reassurance as I am and that actors are, if anything, more fearful than writers. I have come to love the vulnerability of actors, the visual brilliance of directors. But then I knew nothing. I thought they were judging me when in fact they were terrified I was judging *them*.

We flew home on the red-eye to a dismal dawn in New York. I never return home without Frank Sinatra's version of "New York, New York" playing in my head. But I was no longer sure where my home was. Wasn't it with Jon? Was it with Henry?

For the next few months, I lived with Allan but kept up a clandestine correspondence with Jon. I have saved the letters for Molly—if she ever decides she wants to read them. Probably not till she's fifty, and who knows if I'll be around by then. If I am, I'll be eighty-six, and even though I come from a long-lived family who can say what I'll remember, if anything. My family is also famous for memory loss.

Since the fundamentalist Christians are awaiting the Rapture and the Misleader-in-Chief is armed with nuke-u-lar bombs (and is enough of a dry drunk to use them), *none* of us may be around.

If you are, Molly—and I pray you will be—please read them laughingly and be kind. Without them, you wouldn't be here.

. . .

Julia and I continued our endless transcontinental conversations. Jon and I secretly talked all night—from midnight (when Allan was asleep and it was 9 p.m. in L.A.) till three. After eight years of marriage to someone "who talked like a telegram—as if the words cost money," as my grandfather said, these conversations were balm to the loneliness in my marriage.

What did Allan think? What did he feel? To my shame, I never even considered him. Perhaps if I had, I wouldn't have been able to leave.

There was no question that as soon as Jon found a house for us to rent, I'd take off. Maybe I didn't know it, but all my close friends did.

Deep in the recesses of my brain, I was trying to choose between Hollywood bling and the life of the noiseless, patient writer flinging filaments out of herself, hoping they'll catch somewhere. I was making a choice and I didn't even know it.

It was January before Jon and I (still not divorced from Dr. Jong) moved to Malibu, to a rented house at

25321 Old Malibu Road (left turn at the Malibu Pharmacy, where you got your meds, and proceed up the beach road till you come to the end). On a rise opposite the houses directly on the beach, we lived on a short street populated by middlingly successful rock musicians, struggling screenwriters and out-of-work actors who had always wanted to live "at the beach." It was the first time in my life that I lived where most of the people stumbled out to their mailboxes at ten or eleven wearing their terry-cloth robes. *Nobody* had a real job. It was reassuring.

Waking up to hear the Pacific crashing haunts me. Last summer we rented a house in Santa Barbara in part because I wanted to relive those Malibu pleasures and Malibu is too built up now. I love Montecito and Big Sur and would happily alight in either place were it not that my loves live here, in the frantic city of my birth. I will probably perch in New York like a pigeon on a ledge till the floods come and the ocean rises to my terrace on the twenty-seventh floor. Remind me to bring my dinghy. It may be our only way out after the fault under the East River trembles and the sea level rises.

So I became a Malibuvian and wrote poems about the Pacific with its wildness, its red tides and its passing whales. I saw Julia intermittently, but the movie seemed stalled, which is not unusual for movies. Most writers can write half a dozen novels in the time it takes to go from the option to the movie, if indeed it's ever made. My father used to tell me I was lucky because all I needed was "a pencil and a blank piece of paper." He was right. It takes an army to make a film, while it only takes one monomaniac to write a novel. This is the purest freedom.

Our rented house had a large open-air central atrium and snakes occasionally slithered out—as well as scorpions and the occasional intrepid mouse. It was not what people imagine when they say "Malibu," but we were in love so everything was delicious.

Once, we were banished from the house by a major plumbing crisis—nothing flushed—and we moved to Henry's in Pacific Palisades. That was when I began audiotaping his recollections of the Paris years, which sound just like the voice of his books.

I would commute back to Malibu Road to see the progress of our plumbing problem and I would run into our landlord, Harry, a disheveled, gray-haired native

Angeleno from Hancock Park who never ceased to be amazed by the tackiness of the beach house he'd inherited.

"They built 'em on these concrete slabs, never thinking they'd be more than beach shacks. Sometimes they brought in the studio carpenters to do it. So they just sank the plumbing in concrete—and never even left a plan for where it was. That's why we gotta jackhammer up the whole floor." He pointed to the stinking ditch dividing our bedroom from our living room. It was filled with sewage. I studied it, thinking how I would describe it to Henry. Then I drove back to Pacific Palisades.

It may have been around the time we were living with Henry that Mario Puzo invited me to dinner. He was living in Malibu briefly and we met somewhere—I forget where. We ate at a Chinese restaurant in Santa Monica that looked like a Las Vegas club.

"So whatcha doing next?

"Writing my second novel."

"A real mistake. They'll never forgive you."

"But if I don't write the second novel, how can I write the third?"

"Fahget it. Write movies—that's where the money is.

Ya know how much they're payin' me for *The Towering Inferno*?"

"No idea."

"Seven-fifty—and they'll probably never use the script. I don't care. I've turned the money over to my sister already. To pay off her house. It's like printing money. But a second novel—they'll kill you. They *always* kill second novels."

"That's why I have to get through it and get to the third."

"You're nuts. I'll introduce you to my agent. Take the money and run. You think anyone cares about books? Who has time to read in this rat race?"

"You're probably right."

"You know it. I'm right. I was poor a long time. I'll never be poor again." He took another mouthful of Peking duck.

"You sound like Scarlett O'Hara."

"You could do worse," Mario said. "Besides, you're a dame. Dames always get the short end of the stick."

So I struggled with my second novel with Mario's prophecy in my ears. We moved back to Malibu eventually and dealt with the imperfect plumbing.

Then one day, I picked up some tabloid and read that Julia Phillips, producer of *The Sting,* was planning to direct *Fear of Flying.* She was in a director's workshop at the American Film Institute and she was quoted as saying that she understood the material better than any male director and there was no reason she couldn't direct it herself. What happened to Schlesinger, Ashby, Donen? The author of the book is always the last to know.

I was devastated by this news. I didn't know how far Julia's drug use had gone or how much her megalomania was fueled by coke, but I knew she had promised a great, experienced director. I didn't know that those Hollywood riffs—*we'll get him, we'll get her* and *we'll get them*—were meaningless. I hadn't even seen Julia for a while and I thought she was avoiding me. The truth was she had become more and more unhinged by drugs. I never knew this till much, much later.

I was seething. I should have just crept away and forgotten the film. I should have written my second novel or called Mario's agent—or called Mario, for that matter. I probably would now. But Julia had seduced me, suckered me, romanced me with dreams of a great film, and now she'd left me flat. I consulted an ancient Hollywood lawyer whose office was in Century City and whose desk was on a raised platform even higher than

Louis Nizer's. (The exalted platform is the revenge of short lawyers.)

"There's nothing you can do. The names of those directors are not written into any contract. Besides, the book writer is the least important person in making the movie. They own it. What they do with it is not your business. Do yourself a favor and move on."

His advice was good and I should have taken it. Unfortunately, I met the Christian and his lions.

Noel Marshall was a former Hollywood talent manager who had produced *The Exorcist* and wanted to score again with something bigger. He had wild white hair and spoke with the conviction of a televangelist. He was married to the beautiful Tippi Hedren and they lived in a house nearest the wildest of canyons—Franklin—with a beautiful cheetah. Once, when I stayed with them, the cheetah came into the guest room and stared at me all night, crouching as if about to pounce. Cheetahs are the fastest animals on earth. Noel insisted this one was tame.

"The Egyptian pharoahs walked them on golden leashes. They were kept as pets."

Occasionally, the most beautiful girl in the world visited. It was Tippi's daughter, Melanie Griffith, then in her teens and already involved with Don Johnson. She was the loveliest creature I had ever seen. Her skin kissed her bones with the radiance Monet bestowed on his cathedrals. Tippi, in those days, commuted to Guatemala, where she was saving victims of earthquakes. Noel remained in L.A.

I wish I could remember who introduced me to Noel, but in those days people were constantly calling me to say, "You must meet my friend." Sudden fame makes you popular in ways you may not have experienced before. And I never *thought* I was famous, so I always believed these people wanted to be friends. I was Ms. Gullibility. New notoriety is no place to make new friends.

A lot of the new "friends" wanted me to write a "really tasteful" erotic movie. Or they wanted me to have a "really tasteful erotic talk show." Even I could see through that. But Noel wanted me and Jonathan to meet his lions. That seemed innocent enough.

So we drove out to Palmdale in the desert. There, in a cyclone-fenced preserve, with caves and savannahs and cliffs within, there lived a pride of lions that were to star in Noel's forthcoming movie, *Roar!*

Jon and I watched speechlessly as Noel went in among the lions, roared and raised his hands at the big yellow lioness, cuddled her cubs and walked among the others with all the insouciance of an ancient Christian who knows he has God's blessing. He greeted them all by name, tickled them behind the ears as if they were just big Labradors and emerged triumphant from their midst, saying, "Now you try it."

At that point in my life I would try anything—the more self-destructive the better—but with lions I hesitated. Then Noel explained to us that he had bought them because, in trying to film his movie about a family whose dream was to save lions in the wild, he'd discovered that the trainers were more difficult than the beasts. They fought among themselves, were political and conniving, making it impossible for him to shoot the movie, which was to star Tippi and Melanie and himself. He had been working on the movie for at least a decade. It was a labor of love. He believed that it would be the ultimate statement about man and beast, man and God, and that it would change the course of environmentalism and therefore history.

We talked about lions. Jon and I stalled before entering the lions' den. Noel theorized about the training of wild beasts and the necessity to roar at them, never show fear and appear to be taller than they. He promised it was perfectly safe to go among them. Still, we hesitated.

Noel was a showman, the Belasco of Palmdale, but Jon and I were writers. Noel goaded. We hung back.

"The only thing to fear is fear itself," Noel announced, as if he had invented the phrase. "Fear is the enemy. Fear is not your friend. Fear is how the world beats you. Conquer fear and you conquer everything. It's perfectly safe."

And to make his point, he went in again and brought out two cuddly lion cubs, which he put in our arms, smelling of the pungent wild but soft as kittens. The cubs were happy to nestle in our arms while Noel snapped Polaroids. Then he suggested we go in.

Convinced by his charisma, we did tiptoe into the den for a few moments, posed with the lioness and her cubs and exited fast, trying not to show fear.

Later, when we showed the Polaroids to Howard and Bette Fast, they had the desired effect.

"Are you kids insane?" Howard asked. And Bette, pale anyway, blanched.

How we got from the lions' den to Noel's lawyer filing a lawsuit on my behalf against Julia and Columbia Pictures on the grounds of fraud is all a blur.

"We'll file the suit, they'll give us the rights back and then we'll make the movie," Noel said. It was sorta like:

"We'll go into Iraq and the people will throw rose petals at our feet."

Of course the opposite happened. Columbia, then run by David Begelman—"the old riverboat gambler," as he called himself—was utterly unimpressed by the ploy. Julia was infuriated. The result was years of litigation, a court case that plunged me into a bottomless depression—of course I lost—and legal bills that became astronomical.

American authors have no right to insist on quality films being made of their work. This is not France. We have no *droit moral,* which allows French authors to protest that that an adaptation defiles their work. Noel vanished. The movie was moribund. Jon and I moved to Connecticut, got pregnant and eventually married. And Howard and Bette followed. All we had to show for our folly were a few pictures of us with lions and hundreds of thousands of dollars of legal bills. I have done stupid things in my writing life, but this was the stupidest.

To get as far as I could from the seductions of Hollywood, I decided to write my eighteenth-century romp, *Fanny: Being the True History of the Adventures of Fanny Hackabout Jones.*

It took me five years and it saved my life. Sitting in the

Beinecke Library in New Haven, holding the Boswell Papers in my white-cotton-gloved hand, I came back to myself. No more lions, no more lawsuits, no more snakes slithering out of the foliage. I was back in the safety of the library, dreaming of Fanny becoming a witch, a highwaywoman, a pirate, a high-class courtesan in eighteenth-century London. She was my female Tom Jones, my innocent orphan, seduced into all kinds of terrible trouble, who finally grows up, discovers herself heiress to a great estate, rediscovers her true love, writes her memoirs for her daughter and lives happily ever after—until, of course, John Cleland pinches her life story and distorts it into *Fanny Hill*.

That Molly was born on page four hundred and something, that she had bright auburn hair just like the heroine I'd created, healed me and made me whole.

The novel received a front-page rave in *The New York Times Book Review*. It brought me back to the period I'd loved most in college and graduate school. It reactivated my sense of satire, my ability to laugh, and the balance between writing and private life.

I had closed the door on Hollywood forever. Or so I thought.

. . .

So the movie was never made. Begelman committed suicide; Noel finally made *Roar!* (his wife and step-daughter were mauled in the process); and Melanie became a big star. Chief executives came and went at Columbia. Goldie and Barbra got too old to play the twenty-nine-year-old Isadora. (The tragedy of the actress, according to Strindberg, is growing older.) Women went out of fashion in Hollywood, crept back, then went out of fashion again—at least as subjects for films that would appeal to twelve-year-old boys. The book kept selling anyway, became famous in Croatia, Poland, Korea and Taiwan and was pirated in China. Women in all these disparate places wrote to say they thought that Isadora's story was the story of their lives. I marveled over this—how alike women's feelings were in such different cultures.

Various directors came forward wanting to make the movie, but by then Julia's reputation was dashed and when she rose up threatening suit or demanding millions, they disappeared. Columbia owned it along with a lockerful of other books—by Colette, Saul Bellow and other luminaries—that would never be made. Under American law, a book is like a parcel and once it changes hands that's it.

Your heirs have one moment to take it back—when

you die—but you will never see it made while you're alive.

From time to time there are flurries of interest. I recently learned that the brilliant creator of *Murphy Brown* has written a new script, so maybe there's hope. I see the movie as a period piece of the seventies with seventies music—all seen as a flashback of a mother's life told to her daughter. But I have had to detach from the fate of this book in order to preserve my sanity. I cared too much once. So now I don't want to care at all. It's like a painful divorce that makes you swear off love—at least for a decade.

Julia and I satirized each other in books—which made everything worse. I satirized her as a crass Hollywood coke addict and she told the world I looked like Miss Piggy. None of this helped.

In the thirty years that went by, there was no charity or empathy between us, but every time I was in Los Angeles, I wanted to call her. I was just too scared.

We had unfinished business. We had fallen in love, then fallen in hate, and now it was time for something new. I had come out to the Coast to promote one of my books and tape *Politically Incorrect* and speak at UCLA. I was staying with my brother and sister-in-law in Bel Air and I had a day off, so I screwed up my courage and called Julia.

She was happy to hear from me, invited me to her apartment in West Hollywood, and I went.

When I knew her, Julia had lived like a Hollywood princess. Now she was down on her luck. The house in Coldwater Canyon was gone, the husband was gone, the daughter was grown.

I came into a rather gaudy black-mirrored apartment near Sunset Strip.

We looked at each other. Then we hugged for a long time. She smelled of cigarette smoke and so did the whole place.

"I have an amend to make," I said, when we moved apart. "I was wrong. I should never have sued you. I broke your heart and also broke my own. It was really a stupid and nasty thing to do. I was in a rage and I didn't know what to do. It all seems so meaningless now."

"I understand amends. I've been in and out of so many rehabs you wouldn't believe it."

"I believe it. I've been through hell with my daughter. Not to mention my own stuff."

"I stopped the coke—but the smoking I swear I will stop soon. I'm down to one pack a day. A little wine. That's it."

"What happened here?" I looked around the garish apartment.

"None of it's my stuff. My taste is better than this crap. Lost the house, but I'm working my tail off." Her voice was very hoarse. "I'm working on a project with Matt Drudge. He's not a bad guy. Much better than you think. Not dumb."

And then we sat down and regaled each other with love stories, divorce stories, stories about our daughters.

Warily, we crept up on *Fear of Flying*.

"Your script wasn't a piece of shit. It had possibilities. I shoulda given you more guidance. I was a mess in those days, I thought you knew. I thought everybody would forgive me. I was wrong. Spielberg threw me off the set of *Close Encounters*. None of the guys could stand me because I saw straight through them. Then my lawyer blew his brains out, then David Begelman."

"Drugs?"

"Who the fuck knows?"

"After *You'll Never Eat Lunch* and Spielberg dropping me, it was downhill all the way. I guess it's not smart to crap where you eat."

"I did it too," I said.

"We weren't allowed to make mistakes like the guys were. They just keep failing upwards. Remember feminism? Hah. Nothing's changed."

"Well, a few things—but not like we thought."

"It was the times. It was the drugs," she said.

"The sex," I said.

"The feeling we were immortal."

"I never felt immortal," I said.

"I did. I wish I could get that back."

Julia and I exchanged some funny e-mails. She was looking for the first and second scripts of *Fear of Flying*. We were going to work together again. We would make it all O.K. She signed her e-mails "Jools." I signed mine "E." Then there was a long silence. She was going for medical tests. They were a pain. She was sure they were nothing. Then silence.

About six months later, I woke up one morning and found her obituary in *The New York Times*. It was a kind obituary. Her intelligence was noted. Her bad reviews were not quoted. She'd had cancer. She was gone.

IV.

DOES WRITING TRUMP FAMILY?

I am going to write because I cannot help it.

CHARLOTTE BRONTË

I grew up in a family of depressives. My grandfather used to say that the artist "carried the dead weight of the world on his shoulders." The artist (could he have also meant the *Übermensch*?) toiled forward with heavy steps, groaning in pain like an Egyptian slave building a pyramid in a Cecil B. DeMille movie, scored by Dmitri Tiomkin or Elmer Bernstein, and managed to move that block of stone a half inch. Then came the cruel over-seer to flog him back into the pit of darkness. Or something like that. By my grandfather's definition, all talented people were born to labor in futility. My grandfather was Russian. And Jewish. But is that enough to explain it?

All the Jews of the Pale must have been marrying their cousins for generations—which to me explains not only the glut of Ashkenazic genetic diseases—like Tay-Sachs and Canavan's—but also the epidemic of depression. Woody Allen's great-grandparents and mine—not to mention Philip Roth's—sat around saying "The Cossacks are coming" for so long that their offspring had no choice but to tell jokes. Or die. The ones who survived alternated their depression with bitter humor.

Who but an Eastern European Jew could make up the fantasy of a writer in hell doomed to toss his pages into the fiery pit as soon as he writes them? The fantasy is Isaac Bashevis Singer's—but it could have been my grandfather's or Woody Allen's or Philip Roth's or Cynthia Ozick's or mine. Futile it may be, but you have to keep doing it. Why? To ward off depression. Writing is tough, but it's a lot less tough than depression. Which basically leads to suicide. Unless you make a joke.

Writing is the first antidepressant. It came before Prozac or Effexor. And it was cheaper. All you needed was a blank piece of paper and a pencil, as my father used to say. If you were lucky, you might even make some dough. But even if you didn't, you were doing something godlike—emblazoning words of fire on a tablet of stone and handing them to Moses, any Moses. So what if there were a lot of "shalt nots"? Interestingly enough, just writing "shalt not" cheered you up.

No wonder Henry Miller called writers "ingrown toenails" and preferred hanging out with painters.

I think writing elevates my mood because it's a way of imposing order on chaos. Eudora Welty said in her memoir, *One Writer's Beginnings,* that in order to tell a story you have to find sequence in experience. Sequence is a way of understanding an experience that has previously been obscure. Of course you will inevitably distort your memories by sequencing them, but memory is already distorted when you retrieve it. Memory is always impure. We tend to make up narratives for ourselves that grow stronger with each retelling. Of course they depart from what really happened because what really happened was not fixed in language. Whatever is not fixed in language drifts away. Once we create a narrative, the underlying events diffuse like fog. A great deal of ink has been wasted on autobiography versus fiction, when the truth is that all autobiography is fiction and all fiction is autobiography. The important thing to remember is that we are narrative-making creatures. In making a narrative, one always employs choice.

Anyway, if you think of writing as something you are doing to cheer yourself up—and to cheer other people up—who cares about purity? Sometimes I think the only happy writers are the ones who think of themselves as entertainers.

Ken Follett is like this. He entertains, but he never lowers his standards. He is very successful and he takes his work seriously and never does less than his best. His research is impeccable. He begins each book by writing a very detailed outline. The first outline is rather rough-hewn. The subsequent ones are more and more detailed. They include everything about characters, setting and plot progress. The outlines are rewritten and expanded until they become detailed patterns for the book. Then he writes it, staying as close to the outline as possible.

Of course there are surprises along the way, but Follett likes them to be small craftsmanlike surprises. He tries to put himself in the reader's place and plan the most surprise in the reader by having the least surprise in the writer. He is not a depressive. In this way, he writes worldwide best-seller after worldwide best-seller.

To outline or not to outline—that is the question. I think a plot-driven novel probably should be outlined, while a character-driven one needs more freedom. I can't outline. I start with a character and her predicament, and go from there. Plot is not my forte.

I never know the arc of the story until I am at least a third of the way into the novel. If I have realized my character sufficiently, she will give me my plot. Plot is just a fancy way of saying *"and then."*

Jorge Luis Borges claimed all fantastic literature had only four plots: the mingling of dream and reality, the double, time travel and the book within the book. You could spend your whole writing life on these four and Borges did. So has Umberto Eco—and others too numerous, as they say, to mention.

Once, in a rare-book store, I came upon a book called *Plotto,* which detailed all the possible plots in literature and how to combine them. It seems to me like a project a would-be writer would tackle instead of writing a novel. There was a lot in *Plotto* about killing the king or queen, babies switched at birth and magic spells. The truth is that no plot device will save you if your characters are not believable. And if they are, you can get away with practically anything.

"There are three rules for writing novels," Somerset Maugham said; "unfortunately, nobody knows what they are."

The greatest problem of novel writing for me is to believe in the book long enough for it to reveal its secrets. As the writer, I am hardly the best person to know whether I have cast my spell of enchantment on the reader. I go on pure nerve. I have to assume that the reader is bewitched. In order to believe this, I have to be bewitched myself. When the spell breaks, there is always the chance I will take the manuscript out to the incinerator—as Nabokov is said to have done with *Lolita*.

Vera Nabokov, however, pulled it out. Or so the story goes. It may also be a fiction devised by Vera and Vlodya to embellish his reputation. Never trust a writer—not even a dead one.

A few years ago, I took my daughter Molly to see where I lived when I was beginning my first real self-education as a writer. It was a dismal Army housing project in Heidelberg with mustard-colored walls and sad rectangles of dried grass between the buildings.

"I can't believe you ever lived in such a *dump*," Molly said. "Where did you write?"

"I wrote in the second bedroom of a two-bedroom apartment with ugly gray Army-issue furniture. It was a fourth-floor walk-up."

We had come back to Heidelberg to participate in a documentary for German TV about writers who had lived in Heidelberg—like Goethe. But there was nothing picturesque about the place I'd lived.

Molly and I trudged up to the fourth floor and rang the bell. I explained to the harried lady of the house that I had once lived there and she let us in to the squalor. The same dirty oversized furniture. Toys, boots and clothes everywhere. The second bedroom was not much different from my memories of it. The boxy desk. The day-bed. The depressing view of the muddy courtyard. But it was here that I had written the first hurried riffs for *Fear of Flying*. I had scribbled in my notebook "The History of the World Through Toilets"—never dreaming it would find its way into a novel. I had studied Denise Levertov's poems, trying to figure out why she broke her lines where she did. I had discovered Anne Sexton and Sylvia Plath and realized that a woman's daily life could be the material for poetry. I had written poems and stories never dreaming they would ever be read by anyone.

"What a horrible place," Molly said. "Let's go." She wanted to get back to our fancy hotel downtown and play video games. Nostalgia is never what your children want from you. They want absolute love, and unwavering support. They want omnipotence—until the

curtain blows aside and you are revealed as the Wizard of
Oz. I hated seeing my father's weakness at the end of his
life. When I dream of him now, he is always in his prime.
The old man has vanished; the young man is immortal.

In Heidelberg, I remembered what a sanctuary this
dreary housing project had been to me. Far away from
family, graduate school and the chaos of my family in
New York, I had found a cocoon in which to educate
myself as a writer. From the outside, it was dreary. In my
memory, it was the oasis in which I blossomed. I wasn't
anybody then. I was Erica Mann, age twenty-three, wondering if she could write anything worth reading. But
there were no expectations weighing me down, either. I
look back at that time and realize how utterly free I was.

Molly and I did go back downtown to the elegant
hotel suite where the TV producers were putting us up.
We were photographed all over the picturesque old town
as if the cobblestones and curved bridges and ancient
Schloss were what made Heidelberg inspiring. I don't
know about Goethe, but Heidelberg nurtured me because it was there that I was left alone to read and
write. It had nothing to do with the *Schloss* or the *Alte
Brücke*.

There is in writing—or any creative work—a kind of

fuck-you impulse. Part of the energy comes from sheer rebelliousness. *I'll show you!* a writer says. *I am not who you think I am.* Sometimes you have to get mad just to begin. You think you are all alone in this—but battalions of dead writers who faced the same challenge are shouting in your ears. (Margaret Atwood calls writing "negotiating with the dead.") You have to drown them out when they keep you from hearing yourself. They are alternately encouraging and stifling. You have to invent a voice that will make all their voices obsolete. You can't do this without grit, aggression, a kind of madness. No one really asks for a new book, but you need to write it. And your need will eventually infect your reader.

If you want to be a nice person, don't write. There's no way to do it without grinding up your loved ones and making them into raw hamburger. It's hard to do it and keep a social schedule. The essential chapter will sometimes arrive on the night of a dinner party. Your job is to be always ready. Writing is not a life. It is, as Graham Greene said in the title of his autobiography, "a sort of life."

I work most happily when I have nothing on my schedule, when I am in my Connecticut house alone with no need to go anywhere but for a walk or a swim. And

I love writing in friends' houses where the telephone calls are not for me, or rented houses in different time zones. One reason Venice was productive for me was the six-hour time change from New York. By the time anyone phoned from New York, I was out swimming or walking. Yet I'm a gregarious creature. I don't want to escape all the time. And how can I be a satirist without going to parties where all the hypocrisies we live by are exposed?

For me, writing a novel is never a linear process. Sometimes it takes years of meandering, wandering around the world and writing pages to be tossed away.

Fear of Flying began originally in a very different way than it now does. In fact, it was an entirely different book—narrated by Isadora's first husband, the madman—based, of course, on my first demon and my first husband. I got just so far in it and I realized that this character was a pastiche of all the Nabokovian narrators I had loved. So I stopped and had no idea how to begin again. In the meantime, I wrote poetry. It was in poetry that I developed the courage to write in the voice of a woman.

When I had enough poems for a book, I began send-

ing the manuscript around to various contests that promised first-book publication. For a number of years my manuscript came close, but no cigar. So about three years into the process, I sent the book to a bunch of university contests and one commercial publisher. And that was when Holt, Rinehart and Winston (as it was then called) picked up my first book of poems, *Fruits & Vegetables,* and published it, in 1971.

My first publisher, Aaron Asher, wanted a novel, of course. (In those days of yore, publishers actually published *poetry* hoping for novels.) So I showed him my Nabokovian pastiche, then called *The Man Who Murdered Poets*. It was a doppelgänger story about a mediocre poet who murders a great poet because he believes he can take on his powers that way.

"This is a publishable novel," he said, "but I won't publish it and someday you'll thank me. Why are you writing in the voice of a male madman?"

I didn't tell him all the things that raced through my head—but the truth was that basically I thought nobody would be interested in a woman's point of view.

"Go home," he said, "and write a novel in the irreverent female voice of those poems."

It was just the kick in the ass I needed at that time.

. . .

I'm often asked how my family reacted to my writing. My father was proud of my fame. My mother told me I was writing her obituary. And neither of my sisters has ever quite forgiven me for being a writer. Any writer has to be tough enough to take the condemnation of family. My older sister says, "You should have waited till we all were dead." No use to say, "But then I would have been dead myself." The dead can do many things. Writing is not one of them.

It's not unusual for different family members to have different views of the family history. If you're the writer, you're the one with the ability to assert your point of view in print. If you're funny, it's always at someone's expense. Humor is never benign. Of course the other members of the family will take issue with your viewpoint. How can they not? Perhaps this why my daughter boycotts my books. She wants me as Mom, not as a writer. This is understandable. And now that I have a writer daughter, what a perfect revenge on my own writing life! Reading her, I feel like all the people and events in my life have been put into a Mixmaster, whirled around by fierce blades and spiced with whole chiles. The mother in her first novel goes to Europe instead of taking her addicted daughter to rehab. Do I resent that? No. That is her narrative not mine. Molly must have felt terribly alone—despite the fact that I was there—and she objectified this in the character of the mother. Writers do that. I've done it myself.

I realize it's a compliment to have a daughter who followed in my footsteps. She has her own ironic voice and she completely twists and exaggerates events we shared—but hey, that's what writers do. She writes non-fiction that's as fictional as anything I've ever read. She has a way of showing the absurdities and hypocrisies of human nature, and for me that is more important than my petty ego.

"Did you write the stuff about . . . ?" She pantomimes drinking from a bottle and driving at the same time.

"Don't you *dare* write about that before I do!"

"I'm so jealous," she says. "How come I was never arrested for drunk driving? It's such a good career move—jail."

Until that moment, I have been ashamed. Now I'm hysterical.

"Look what it did for good old Martha."

"True."

"I want that story."

"So do I."

This is the absolute limit of my maternal generosity. She cannot have my drunk-driving experience!

Three months after my father died, in 2004, I wound up in jail. Needless to say, I had never been in jail before. The thought of sleeping on a plastic pad under wincing fluorescent ceiling lights in a glass-fronted cell with one stainless steel toilet (behind cinder blocks) would have been inconceivable to me. So how did I manage to wind up in the drunk tank of the Beverly Hills jail two days before Mother's Day?

My wrists were swollen and bruised by handcuffs applied deliberately tightly by the B.H. police —a three-member team consisting of two mild male policemen and one bitter bitch, who, upon hearing me call for my lawyer before deciding to take a blood test—would the needle give me AIDS?—or a Breathalyzer—would I get pneumonia from the Breathalyzer?—decided to tighten the steel wire cuffs until I bled ("I'm puttin' ya down as refusin' the test," the policewoman said).

"I haven't refused. I just want my lawyer."

"That's not an option in California," she said. "You've refused." And then she scribbled her report.

Presently, the three of them hustled me into a patrol car and sped me off into the night, leaving my rental car with all my stuff in it and my wrists stinging.

As we drove off, I heard the policewoman say, "She's on stuff." I knew this was not true—unless you counted the Effexor I had just started and the wine at dinner with old friends I grew up with in New York, who were now television moguls.

Was I still attracted to oblivion? Was I more like Plath and Sexton than I liked to admit? Was I distraught over my father's death? Probably all these things. After a year in which my father died, my daughter got married and had a son, and my sisters hired lawyers to fight over the family fortune, I hardly *needed* to be on stuff. My beloved agent had just revealed he had leukemia. My husband had survived an aortic aneurysm and was alive only by the grace of God. My world had suffered an earthquake far stronger than those that make the chandeliers tinkle on this coast—and here I was standing on painted footprints in the cellar of the Beverly Hills police department, watching my jewelry inventoried, the emerald and diamond engagement ring labeled "white metal with green stone and white stones," my dollars and euros counted along with my bank cards and my Cartier watch with the purple alligator band.

"Carteeyer," the clerk said, counting and recounting my credit cards. She was nice, asked if I wanted a chicken sandwich or apple juice and did not appear to wonder how a woman with such a humongous emerald wound up in the drunk tank. "The Green Lantern" my daughter calls it.

"I haven't read your books, but I'll try to catch them now," she said sweetly, leaving me to wonder how a DUI made me somehow more readable. "And I love that other one—you know—Ms. Danielle is it?"

I nodded. I wasn't about to quarrel with anything after my rough treatment with the cuffs.

Shall I describe the prison-cell floor, the flimsy cotton blanket for a pillow, the plastic bedroll and cotton cover, the clock moving through its interminable intervals adding up to the statutory eight hours?

I had been on television that day arguing with a right-wing talk-show host who claimed that Iraqi prisoners were not *really* tortured in Abu Ghraib.

"What is 'really tortured'?" I asked. "If I attached electrodes to your testicles, you might call it torture."

Now, six hours later, I was in lockup.

Just having your freedom taken away and having to stand on painted footprints is humiliation enough—without hoods, dog leashes and electric shocks. My self-inflicted pain is not vaguely comparable to what our government inflicts on so-called enemy combatants, but it made me aware of the mortification of imprisonment, any imprisonment.

Though I can normally sleep anywhere, I could not sleep away the eight hours.

My dad had been talking to me ever since he died three months before. What would he say now?

"This too shall pass"?

"All you need is a pencil and a blank sheet of paper"?

I suddenly saw his mouth as it was in his coffin, twisted by the undertaker into a crooked scowl.

"Can't you fix his mouth?" I asked the funeral director. "It doesn't look like his expression."

"The best we could do," he whispered. "I'm sorry for your loss," he said robotically. I kissed my father on his icy forehead, leaving a pink-lipsticked two-lip print with which he was buried. I had to kiss him before he was buried. I had to leave my mark. Even that way I had to preempt my sisters.

As I got back to New York, I went back to AA. I had been sober before, sometimes as long as years, and I loved the clarity it gave me.

I did it again, in tribute to my dad and in defiance of my demon. But the State of California was not satisfied with AA. It wanted me to go to an "approved program" for my rehabilitation from a first DUI. So after months of searching and being abstinent and attending AA meetings every day, I found a program at a rehab in New York City that met the California standard. It was not an AA-based program but was based on "harm reduction" therapy. The great state of California blessed it, so I went.

My group included a male heroin addict with long red fingernails (to match his long red hair) and dangling earrings, a college student on weed, a young woman addicted to Percodan and other prescription drugs. Everyone in the group was still using and rationalizing it to the therapist by saying they were using less than before. Nobody aspired to abstinence.

The male heroin addict spoke first. He was the sort of tall man who seemed folded like a portable umbrella when he sat. He was all angles and crooks. "So I did one line last night and then I stopped."

"How did it make you feel?" the therapist asked.

"O.K. I felt I was in control."

"You can't be in control," Ms. Percodan said. "That's impossible."

"But I am."

"I did a little weed," the college student said.

"How do you feel?" the therapist asked.

"O.K."

There was also an old hippie with long gray hair and a Rolling Stones T-shirt.

"I think I know who *you* are," he said.

I didn't answer.

They went around the circle. I had been abstinent for nine months since the DUI, but I was somehow ashamed to say so.

"What about you?" the therapist asked me.

"I find it easier not to drink."

"You're not doing that AA crap, are you?" This from the collapsible man with the red nails.

"It's not crap," said Ms. Percodan.

"Old hat," said red nails.

"I think we must have respect for how others handle their compulsions," said the therapist.

I never went back to that group. But how I handled my addiction is fodder for another book. I will probably not write it, because I know that AA triumphalism is a sure recipe for falling off the wagon. There are some things that are surely beyond words.

Never say never, but I will never drink and drive again. I will never forget to turn my headlights on—as I did that night. I will never drive a car without a GPS, because I can get lost even in Connecticut where I've lived for thirty years, or New York where I was born and raised. I will never try to walk a straight line in pink kid mules. I will never count from a hundred to one backwards.

But how can I keep Molly from writing about my DUI if she wants to? You can't prevent your kids from telling their side of the story. And why should we? They are born to supplant us, and whatever gives them the strength to do so is something we should cheer. They are not born to be our clones. They have their own karma. I can think of little more horrifying than raising my own clone.

If we were honest, we'd admit that we'd like our writing relatives to sound like testimonial toastmasters rather than roast masters when they write about us. We'd like to be beautiful, thin, perfectly groomed, wise, wonderful and generous in our relatives' books. But who wants to read about such paragons? Who would believe they existed? Our readers would feel like guests at a benefit dinner when the emcee gets up to praise some chiseling *gonif* for his fine character—when we all know this slob is only being ceremonially ass-kissed because he gave megabucks to some worthy cause as a cover for his thievery.

Nobody wants to read—or write—about perfect people. Perfection is boring. And unbelievable.

It was my curse or blessing to have interesting relatives. They were all smart and talented. But I was the one with the guts to risk disapproval and defeat. Talent is never enough. Talent without guts gets you exactly nowhere. Which is why I am most proud of Molly. She has guts. She has never been afraid to take me on. Or the world.

The connection between courage and writing is causal. Isaac Bashevis Singer begins various first-person stories in the voice of a demon—or even Satan himself. You don't doubt him. You don't say, "How did you go from being a puzzled grown-up Yeshiva boy with feuding mistresses in Brooklyn and the Bronx to being the King of Darkness?" You believe it. You believe it because of the authority in his voice. Author and authority are inevitably linked. You can make anything happen as long as you believe it.

When you're the writer in the house, it's your version

that gets told. Naturally, other people resent that. The problem is that you must live with them and at the same time live with your own demon. The demon says, "The hell with them! Tell the story!" The family says, "Be nice. Don't embarrass us. And, above all, be good to Israel."

There is no way to make peace between these two conflicting demands.

During the two years my father was dying, I'm sure I saw his last days differently from my sisters. I knew he was fading. I'd go over to his house and try to get him out of bed, but he preferred to sleep away the days. When he awoke, he wandered around the house looking lost and pale. He was angry at having to die, angry with everyone who was living, angry with my mother who was still her contentious self.

Before his last operation, I had visited my father in the fancy hotel ward of Mount Sinai. Told he had a blockage in his colon, he was looking forward to the surgery that he imagined would restore his youth. I had seen the same thing with my father-in-law, Selig, who wanted to submit to lung surgery at eighty-three. "Cut it out, cut

it out," they say. But there is an undertone, a minor theme as well.

"Do you know Spanish?" my father asked.

I nodded. *"Poco."*

"La vida es sueño. Life is a dream. I look forward to that deep sleep."

Throughout this book about my life as a writer, there is another book trying to get out. The demon is the midwife. I am trying to make sense of my father's death. He keeps popping into this book wailing, "Remember me!" like Hamlet's father's ghost. "Life is a dream, but the dream disintegrates unless you write it down," he reminds me.

It's been my experience that in every book there's another book trying to get out. Every book is a preparation for the next. This book wants to become a memoir about my father. At the same time, it is cooking up my next novel.

The last year my father was healthy, he insisted on re-telling me the story of his life and having me make notes. He told it punctuated by jumping jacks in the middle of the bedroom floor.

"*'Get a job!'* was all my father ever said. And I always worked," he said, jumping. "If you didn't work you were a bum." (Thump.) "I would go around the neighborhood, looking for signs that said BOY WANTED. I always found something." (Thump.) "I started out playing weddings with Sammy Levinson when I was sixteen. That was already a good job. But you needed equipment. Sammy had a fiddle; I had no drums at first. I bought them with my BOY WANTED jobs. But my father said not to spend money on lessons since I was already making money with no lessons. That was why I wanted all my daughters to have lessons. Education." (Thump.)

"But you can't beat a job that only needs a pencil and blank sheet of paper. A writer. No equipment." (Thump. Thump. Thump.)

To the end, he used his long walks to go into every bookstore and rearrange the books so mine were face out, covering other writers' books.

He was an extremely competitive guy. He never stopped craving. That was why his end was so hard.

I carry on his craving, fighting with myself to detach from craving. I don't think he ever stopped fighting with himself.

At the end, when he was all skin and bones, ninety pounds of wasted body, he could hardly breathe or

speak, but he still had the strength to applaud me silently if I said something he liked. And he could still curse me out if I said something he hated.

As a writer, I am the one making notes by the hospital bed or in the funeral home. I feel ashamed and exhilarated at the same time. Life keeps happening in all its mess and squalor, and I am the one trying to squash it into a box, a book.

When I was a little girl and couldn't imagine life without my family, I used to think that when I grew up I would travel the countryside with all of them—my parents, my grandparents, my sisters—in a round vehicle on wheels, with an ever-replenished refrigerator in the middle and a top open to the sun and stars. In my mind, I called it the "Roundling" (I never shared this fantasy with anyone—as if I knew it was somehow incestuous or forbidden) and in my imagination we were all together forever, traveling in lazy circles through beautiful landscapes, always safe, always fed, always united.

Now my beloved grandparents are dead, my athletic, musical father is astonishingly dead and my unforgettably fierce mother is fading away. My sisters have their own lives, partners and children and troubles, and so do

I. They sometimes act like my worst enemies. This dream of eternal togetherness is outlandish. But if I take myself back to the child I was then, I understand the fantasy of the Roundling as safety, stasis, freedom from sorrow. Nothing changes. Nobody dies. Nobody grows up—or old. Why did I suddenly remember this long-buried fantasy while writing this book? I haven't thought about it since I was a child.

Because writing is an attempt to preserve the past, to keep it safe and hermetically sealed in a sort of time capsule. Writing is the ultimate Roundling, keeping us all young and together forever.

Nobody can write without wanting to bring the past into the present or without wanting to show how the past informs what happens today. The deepest struggle we experience, the struggle that makes us the unhappiest, is the attempt to stop time and keep all our attachments intact. Attachments cause pain. We must learn to detach and writing is the opposite of detachment. Or is it?

I've been fencing with attachment and detachment particularly in the last few months since my father died. I want to write about him, but I don't want to freeze—or murder—him in the pages of a book. For years I thought I understood him, but it was only in the last phase of his life, when he was ill, that I suddenly saw him as a tough

little Jewish boy from Brownsville fighting for his life
with his fists, his wit, his tenacity. I understood why he
was often so stubborn and so hostile under all his
humor. Stubbornness probably saved his life when he
was young.

He wasn't the tallest or the strongest boy, but he was
the most determined. He could shoot baskets as accu-
rately as the tall guys. He could flatten anyone who called
him "kike." He loved the piano, but he was a drummer
to his bones. Sometimes you can't know people till they
are almost dead.

What a fighter my father was! During his last hospi-
talization he tried to escape from the emergency room,
from the ICU and from his hospital suite on the fancy
private floor of Mount Sinai. He was right. It was the
pneumonia he caught in the hospital that would finally
do him in at ninety-two and not any of the three types of
cancer he got and conquered. He seemed to have fore-
knowledge of his demise and struggled like mad to get
away from those resistant germs he knew were awaiting
him. He pulled out breathing tubes, peeing tubes, IVs.
He did not go quietly.

More than once I kept him from getting out of bed.
How could I have done that? Once someone is in the
hospital, he is bound by the iron rules of the institution.

I have always hated institutions and so did my father. In his frenetic exercising twice a day, in his attempt to control his money, his daughters, his sons-in-law, his wife, he was expressing his need for absolute freedom from the rules of others. He lost that freedom at the end.

Sadly, I played my own part in his loss of control. I didn't mean to. He was failing, but now I wish I had let him escape the hospital that killed him.

He never would have had a fantasy of a Roundling. His greatest fantasy was escape. He escaped at the piano, the drums, the basketball hoop. He escaped by exercising, by traveling all over the world, supposedly for his business but really because his temperament required it. He always wanted to get away. I know men are made differently, but he was even more of an escape artist than most men. Why do you think I chased those demons through hotel rooms all over the world?

None of us in that Roundling will ever escape. We should be buried in it together. Because the Roundling is, in fact, a cemetery. It's a sort of pie-shaped burial plot, like the famed Sedgwick pie of Edie Sedgwick's eccentric Massachusetts family.

Arrived at the finish,
unfrightened, unblemished, free

of craving, he has cut away
the arrows of becoming.
This physical heap is his last.

. . .

ungrasping,
astute in expression,
knowing the combination of sounds—
which comes first & which after.
He is called a
last-body,
   greatly discerning
   great man.

That was the poem the mousy male social worker (with the long gray ponytail) from the Palliative Care Team (I called them the Death Squad) quoted to my father in the hospital.

He had studied Buddhism. Detachment? Surely you must be kidding.

"Bullshit!" my father hissed. "Pure unadulterated bullshit."

"But, Mr. Mann, you would be happier if you turned over the decisions to your daughters and gave them permission to—"

"Bullshit!" Then he wanted the little notebook he

carried everywhere with him. He had no energy to read aloud, but he drummed on the page—stabbing it with his index finger:

I feel like King Lear.
I have three daughters
beautiful and dear,
clever and cute,
already in dispute
Who gets more?
Who gets less?
What a terrible mess
for an aging Lear
in geriatric stress.

The social worker was speechless. Nothing—not his M.S.W., nor his Buddhism class—had prepared him for this. He was out of words. We all waited, listening to my father struggle to breathe. "Very nice poem, Mr. Mann," he finally said.

"Bullshit!" said my father. "Get out of here!"

My father started out as a pianist, drummer, bandleader, *tumler,* but *tumler* won. He wound up in business, first as a salesman, then as the founder of his own company.

Because he loved music, worshiped musicians, our house was filled with music. We were dragged to concerts at the Philharmonic every month before we had any idea what a privilege it was. I remember being a bored thirteen and escaping to the ladies' room, where I could practice applying my Powder Pink Revlon lipstick. Bartók or Ives or Beethoven conducted by Dimitri Mitropoulos or Leonard Bernstein would be thundering through Carnegie Hall. What an ingrate I was! My father sent my younger sister to lure me out. I knew I was being an ingrate and I was guilt-ridden. Yet I have grown up with a love of music that mirrors his. I don't play an instrument and I consider myself a troglodyte for this lapse, but music thrills me more than any other art. He gave me this gift.

Our parents' attachments become our own. Often I've thought that if I could have opened my musical of *Fanny Hackabout-Jones* before he died, he would have been prouder of me than for any book I've written. Which is saying a lot. He was proud of me, but he showed this mostly to other people when I wasn't around. He loved to hector me about everything I was doing wrong with my career. I wasn't doing enough PR.

I wasn't hassling my publishers enough. I was too laid back.

Laid back? For most of my life, I have been bedeviled by ambition and professional jealousy (which I counter with defiant generosity like a witch trying to break her own spell). I've only recently learned how to love the work itself without expectation—something he never learned. Perhaps this joy in the work and not the outcome is what is meant by detachment. I achieve it only at rare moments, but when I do my writing flies.

Did he ever know this joy? I doubt it. Nothing was play to him after he became a businessman. Everything was work. Except music.

I started out to be a painter and switched to writing to avoid competing with all the painters in my family. (Probably I also had more talent to write and was freer in using it than if I had gone into the family racket.) But you can't give up seeing the world as a painter does even if you no longer paint. You are doomed to see kaleidoscopes of color in white eggshells and rainbows in black seas.

My reason for giving up painting was cowardly and it goes back to my troubled relationship with my mother.

In my teens, I began to paint colorful rambunctious fantasy portraits that were at odds with all the academic traditions my mother and grandfather held dear. While my mother didn't destroy these canvases, she made it very clear that they were infra dig.

"We used to draw in charcoal first, then in pastels in order to win the *right* to even *use* oil paints. And we never drew from the figure [*figger,* she said in the English manner] till we had mastered plaster casts." The inference was clear: I was jumping in without perfecting my craft.

In the fifties, abstraction was the only permissible language for American art. All the academicians in my family felt threatened. How could I understand that? I was only a kid, looking for my own language in color or words. I wanted to find a language that was neither academic nor abstract, but the world of painting seemed so hemmed in by familial restrictions that I fled to words. Poetry became my refuge. Yet in writing poetry, I was drawn back to the artist's palette of cobalt blue, alizarin crimson, viridian green. I sought flaming watercolor skies.

It's not unusual for whole families to be painters. Think of Tintoretto and his daughter, Marietta Robusti. Or think of the Bellinis—before they became peach-flavored drinks. Or consider Artemisia Gentileschi and her father. Painters tend to grow up in studios. It's possible to see the making of art as a continuum rather than a competition. But in my family, competition was rampant. My grandfather had two talented painter daughters whom he carefully trained, then tried to crush. He would have been much happier as Tintoretto when he could have delegated his daughters to painting angels' wings and folds in satin. In Tintoretto's time, art was still a cooperative enterprise. Many hands were needed to cover immense canvases or ceilings or walls.

By the twentieth century, the idea of the sole genius artist steeped in ego had corrupted everything. By definition, there can only be one genius. The others are reduced to *assistenti*. Especially if they are girls.

We have lost so much by looking at art this way. In fact, all artists stand on the shoulders of their predecessors, just as all writers drown out choruses of the dead.

I was raised to be a fierce competitor, so I must have felt that by competing with my mother I would kill her. Whatever message I was given, my own interpretation was, "Only one of us can paint and live." I withdrew from the field. Better be a writer than commit matricide. But of course I never kissed pictures of painters, so maybe the drive was never there.

Or maybe I lacked the requisite grit for the physicality of painting or sculpture. My early paintings show promise. They are not bad—even though I stopped before I discovered a style. If I was hiding from my own matricidal yearnings, I went on to kill my mother with words. Do all writers kill their parents with their work— then try to resurrect them (as Philip Roth has done in *The Plot Against America*)? The tenderness toward his parents in that book erases the earlier caricatures. They have been dead long enough for him to love them.

When I imagine the painter I might have been, I see myself stretching my own canvases as my grandfather did, and priming them myself. But I imagine much huger canvases than anyone in my family actually painted. What are my subjects? Not horses like Rosa Bonheur's, nor giant sexual blooms like Georgia O'Keeffe's, nor beheaded men like Artemisia Gentileschi's—though these are all images I love. No. My huge canvases are awash with whirling color like the cosmos at the beginning of time. There are exploding suns, clouds of gases, rings of planets that have disappeared. Perhaps I will paint again when my mother dies.

Here the demon enters.

"Why doesn't she die already?"

"I don't want her to!"

"Yes you do! First of all you'll be free of those depressing visits she never remembers you made and you'll get more of her money! Won't that be nice!"

"I don't want her money."

"Liar! You could use it. You're so extravagant. You could buy a house in Italy. How about that? And you could paint there!"

This is absurd. My mother no longer paints. She lies in bed dreaming most of the day and she has forgotten that she ever painted. Why can't I pick up her brush as easily as a tree produces a green shoot? We all grow out of and extend each other. My daughter took to writing as a baby seal takes to swimming. But I think I made her passage easier. I never criticized her work or insisted that she read my own. I never believed that my journey was the only possible journey. I refused to be her critic even when she protested that I was too uncritical, too enthusiastic. I understood that any word of direction from a parent carries the weight of an iron anchor dropping into the sea. It may take the child's enthusiasm with it. A parent can never criticize a child too little. A parent can never encourage too much. Criticism can be found everywhere. The one place you don't need it is at home.

Writing was a way of reinventing my own childhood. I could make it more horrible than it was and heal myself that way. Or I could make it better than it was. Both approaches can be curative. In writing, I had power over the very people who made me feel utterly powerless when I was a child. Even the most horrible childhood can be made tolerable just by writing about it.

I'm thinking of Augusten Burroughs's crazy childhood in *Running with Scissors,* a book I love. Here's a kid whose father deserts him, whose mother is a mad, selfish narcissist and a terrible poet, who is turned over legally to an insane psychiatrist—and yet who thanks his parents at the beginning of the book for giving him the materials of a writer's childhood. He's absolutely right. What would a writer like Augusten Burroughs do with a happy childhood? Nothing. It could have silenced him. Of course he is being tortured with a lawsuit for telling his truth. In another age, he might have been burned at the stake.

I think of my own family *mishegoss,* which I have shamelessly milked for three decades. Or Woody Allen's. Or my daughter's. When I'm being honest, I kneel down and thank God for my crazy parents. I've accepted the fact that we only get so much from parents. The rest we have to provide ourselves. Writing is a way of bringing myself up all over again. I could never have done this as a painter. I must have known intuitively that writing was the only way to live my life.

When we're young, our parents cast these huge shadows. Then they shrink and shrink until it's time to put them in a box. How would I have survived these metamorphoses without writing? And how would Molly have survived without it? Her acid humor is her survival tool. It ate through whatever shadow I cast.

My demon thinks I want to murder my mother. Can he possibly be right? I have often wondered why writers are so obsessed with murder. Is it because we all need to murder our parents in order to go on?

Writers are murderers of more than parents. They murder everyone they love. Time and again I have found that once I have frozen a person in a book I can hardly remember what the real person was like. While writing, I have the sense of having oversimplified, of fixing the character with too few complexities and too many exaggerations—because writing must necessarily be more dramatic than life—but years later I can only remember the person who inspired the character through the scrim of my own words. Everything else about the person is lost to me.

My first husband, for example. I wrote him as "The Madman" in *Fear of Flying* and now that is all I can remember about him. But he was more than just a madman. Who *was* he? The poetry of his schizophrenia was compelling. He thought he was Jesus Christ, but he had done the research. He was a medieval historian, after all. Did I murder the real person for the sake of the fictional one? Is he still alive? Is he still angry with me? We had such a close connection once and now he is only a character frozen in a book.

Last year I had lunch with my first love from high school and sometimes I run into him shopping in the New York neighborhood where we both live. When I see him, I hardly recognize him because he looks so unlike the image in my head and his cameo in *Fear of Flying*. He startles me. Do I want him to stay frozen? Not really. But my nostalgia is more comfortable than the reality. I'm sure that in writing about him, I exaggerated to make him more vivid. That's inevitable. But it knocks off the real person.

When I tell a story at a dinner party, my husband always says, "Remember, this is a story being told by a novelist!" He means I have a tendency to embellish, to make the story more dramatic, to buff up the jokes so they are funnier and shine the dilemmas till they seem symbolic. A storyteller does this naturally, without even being aware of it. My tendency to dramatize murders ordinary life and ordinary people. I care more about drama than ordinary people and ordinary life. I'm lucky to be married to a person who knows this about me and finds it amusing.

Don't hang out with novelists unless you can live with their murdering real life in favor of fiction. Don't be a novelist unless you can tolerate this. It's a short jump from murdering real people to murdering your characters. Most novelists can make that jump for the sake of drama. Novelists always lie about how much it hurts them to murder their characters, but don't believe them. The passage from life to death is the most dramatic of passages, and novelists love it no matter what they say about weeping over their pages. Novelists love to weep.

Why is crime so rampant in novels? Why is murder such a hardy MacGuffin for novelists? Because there's nothing more theatrical. Breaking *any* of the Ten Commandments is good for plotting a novel. But murder and adultery are best. In fact, the more commandments you can break in a single novel, the better.

When I look back on my eight novels so far, I find I

haven't murdered enough people. Death is a great plot device.

The frequency of brutal murder and dismemberment in fairy tales and folk ballads shows us how prevalent these fantasies are. What I fantasize I also fear, because I naturally believe that my foulest fantasies will be turned back against me.

Alan Lomax, the folk historian and collector of traditional ballads, noted that more than half of the folk ballads he collected in America recounted murder, usually the murder of a young woman by a boyfriend.

The interesting thing about folk ballads and fairy tales is that they relate the events of murder with no apologies and no psychologizing. They simply assume everyone will understand that violent behavior is as prevalent, more prevalent in fact, than loving behavior. When we sing Childe ballads or read fairy tales, we are deep in the human unconscious. It's a dark and bloody place.

My grandson was born and my father died within one month of each other. My grandson has my father's father's name. As I watch Max develop, I see in him things I used to see in my father: a delight in clapping his hands as a kind of speech, the soul of a percussionist, a mad desire to climb as high as he can. I don't know what stories Max will tell me, but I have the feeling they will be important ones. I have barely begun to make sense of my father's stories but I believe that if I keep writing about him, I will unravel them. Max is a clean slate, proof that the world is always beginning again. We have complicated conversations in which only two words— "dog" and "car"—are in a common language. Everything else is *lalala* or *deedlee, deedlee*. Yet because I love him so much, I understand him perfectly. If life is a series of intersecting novels, we are only in the prologue. Since I understand everything I love by writing, I will inevitably write about him as I have written about my daughter and as she has written about me. Writing is not a hostile act but an act of understanding—even when it's satirical, even when it's bitter. You only write about the things you care about. Indifference doesn't need to be put into words.

When I was in my twenties, I thought I didn't want to have children because Emily Dickinson and Virginia Woolf didn't have children. What a schmuck I was. I have learned more from Molly than I ever learned from Emily Dickinson and Virginia Woolf. I expect to learn even more from Max, because I've become less self-obsessed.

I had to be dragged kicking and screaming into parenthood, but grandparenthood is easy. I saw him and thought, *Mine*. There was no ambivalence, no anxiety. I always knew he wouldn't stop breathing. I crawl behind him on the rug in perfect bliss. He stops to inspect a toy and I stop to inspect it too. He makes up nonsense words and I make up nonsense words. Hours go by in a sort of trance. It's not that he is so much more interesting than my daughter was at that age, but because my anxiety is gone, I can truly experience him. I can see the world from his point of view. I am in the land of *deedlee*. He has no self-consciousness and I have lost mine.

This was impossible when I was a mother. I was so afraid of being lost in motherhood and angry like my own mother that I fought the dropping of self-consciousness you can experience only with a baby. It's not that I completely lose my adult mind with Max, but I do at moments. When I come back from the land of *deedlee,* I am suddenly struck by his vulnerability and how the Nazis would have snatched him from his mother's arms and killed him. Or killed him in his mother's arms while I watched. And then killed me. Mercifully—

since I wouldn't want to be in a world where he and she were not. My grandson reminds me of the cruelty of the human race. At his briss I worried about letting him be circumcised for fear a new wave of anti-Semitism would doom him. I wanted his penis to be left alone so as not to mark him. So my joy in him is punctuated by sheer terror. This must be how my grandparents felt. Why else would my grandmother have lathered my little hands between hers, saying she was "washing away the Germans"?

When I look at movies of my daughter as a baby, what I see is the openness of her face. She trusts adults to take care of her. She trusts her mother and father. I watch her nod her head loosely then learn to steady it, learn to grab things, learn to sit up, learn to walk, learn to run, I see her growing confidence. All the while I know that when she is four, her parents will separate and her whole world will come apart. I wish I could seize the film and change its ending. I wish I could protect the baby frozen on this film. Yet when she was four, I could not change anything. Nor could her father. I am so pained by this that I eject the disk.

Not long after Molly's father and I separated, I wrote a kid's book about divorce in which everything comes out all right. It was called *Megan's Book of Divorce* and it featured a spunky little girl who never tired of plotting to bring her parents back together. In it, divorce was a sort of lark. The kid got double presents, double toys, double people to spoil her. She was cynical and knowing about the dad's girlfriend and the mom's boyfriend. She played the adults against each other.

I look at the book now and I think it wasn't about Molly at all but about my own wish fulfillment. If I could have really gotten inside Molly's head and dealt with the divorce, the book would have been very dark. But I was trying to make it all O.K.—as much for myself as for Molly. I was trying to rewrite history in the guise of a children's story.

I often do this in writing and don't realize it till years have passed. I cannot bear very much reality. I often wonder how people who don't write endure their lives. At least I can get through the pain by making up stories. Sometimes my funniest stories have come out of the blackest despair.

When I go over to my daughter's house to play with my grandson, I find him surrounded by educational toys. Everything he touches counts, pronounces the names of colors, oinks, moos, neighs, barks or sings in an irritating little electronic voice. He is drowning in didacticism.

What are we so afraid of? Are we afraid these kids won't learn by imitation the way the rest of us did? Why do we need all these Baby Einstein toys? There is a kind of panic inherent in this endless preaching. It's as if we think our children are in danger of whiling away their early years in fantasy. God forbid. Every moment of their lives must be crammed with counting and spelling. I notice that Max's proudest achievement is in finding the little switches that turn these voices off. He is forever turning toys over to probe their mechanical guts. Aha! Rebellion! This generation will surprise us with their reaction to all this motorized talking. Will he disconnect all the robots in sheer fury and read books instead? Already he loves to sit contemplatively and turn the pages of books. We may be surprised by the reaction of this generation to our cramming didactic toys down their throats. I hope so. Play is far more important than drilling. If kids can't play, who can?

This love for didacticism and mistrust of fantasy invades every corner of our culture. It must stem from America's puritanical origins. But when fantasy does creep into children's lives, they are so grateful for it. This accounts for the success of Harry Potter and *The Lord of the Rings*. Children don't need more cramming. Fantasy is what they need.

. . .

In the time I have written and rewritten this book, Max has gone from six months to nearly two. He now calls me in the morning and says, "Hi Erica, Hi Erica, Hi Erica. I love you."

Because I have returned from the odyssey I've described here, I am able to give myself to him completely. Margaret Mead, who was one of my mentors—though I only met her once briefly and knew her chiefly from her books and articles—thought that the way we raise children was of paramount importance to culture. She studied it all her life—whether in New Guinea or the United States. Whenever I see Max exploring his world, I think of her extraordinary understanding of children and our bond with them. She once said that instead of complaining that a child cried so much and kept us from our other work, we should say, "The child smiled so much."

I think back on all the dire predictions that were made in the sixties and seventies—*If women have the birth control pill they'll stop having babies, if women work outside the home their children will be criminals, if women earn money they'll scare away men*—and all of them have proved to be absurd. Women are still wanting babies and having babies. Men have been liberated to be fathers. Children are still hypnotizing their mothers and fathers, grandmothers and grandfathers. The world has not stopped. What I have learned is that the fearmongers are usually wrong about change. It's wonderful to have lived long enough to see it.

"How was the Toddler Center?" I ask Max, who now goes up to Barnard one afternoon a week to play with other toddlers. We are in my study, where I have a huge toy train set waiting for him. He is engrossed by the toy trains, making them crash and fall all over the floor.

I make long lines of trains and he proceeds to pick them up and drop them as though he were King Kong. He is not interested in talking to me about school or anything that is not here and now. All he wants to do is play with trains. But he is entranced with naming.

"Ok-y-pus," he says, picking up the aquarium car with the octopus inside.

"Zebra," he says, lifting the car with the zebra that pops up.

"Ga-raff," he says looking at the car with the tall giraffe.

He is naming the animals and then gleefully dropping the trains on the floor. No sooner do I put the trains together than he picks them up and scatters them on the floor.

"Gold," he says of the train with the golden load.

"Apples!" he says of the orchard train with its fruit. And then he tries to bite the plastic apples, as if to tell me that he knows what they are.

"Choo-choo train!" he shrieks triumphantly, dropping the red engine, which goes on whirring even though it's on its back like an insect.

"All done!" he concludes, having wrecked the trains I carefully assembled.

The love of words is clearly in his genes. The story is not over yet.

ABOUT THE AUTHOR

Erica Jong is the author of nineteen books of poetry, fiction and memoir, including *Fear of Flying,* which has more than 18 million copies in print worldwide. Her most recent essays have appeared in *The New York Times Book Review* and *Elle*. She is currently working on a novel featuring Isadora Wing, the heroine of *Fear of Flying,* as a woman of a certain age. Erica and her lawyer husband live in New York City and Connecticut. Her daughter, Molly Jong-Fast, is also an author.